WA 1249385 6

LEARNING IN SCHOOL, HOME AND COMMUNITY

ICT for Early and Elementary Education

IFIP - The International Federation for Information Processing

IFIP was founded in 1960 under the auspices of UNESCO, following the First World Computer Congress held in Paris the previous year. An umbrella organization for societies working in information processing, IFIP's aim is two-fold: to support information processing within its member countries and to encourage technology transfer to developing nations. As its mission statement clearly states,

IFIP's mission is to be the leading, truly international, apolitical organization which encourages and assists in the development, exploitation and application of information technology for the benefit of all people.

IFIP is a non-profitmaking organization, run almost solely by 2500 volunteers. It operates through a number of technical committees, which organize events and publications. IFIP's events range from an international congress to local seminars, but the most important are:

- The IFIP World Computer Congress, held every second year;
- open conferences;
- working conferences.

The flagship event is the IFIP World Computer Congress, at which both invited and contributed papers are presented. Contributed papers are rigorously refereed and the rejection rate is high.

As with the Congress, participation in the open conferences is open to all and papers may be invited or submitted. Again, submitted papers are stringently refereed.

The working conferences are structured differently. They are usually run by a working group and attendance is small and by invitation only. Their purpose is to create an atmosphere conducive to innovation and development. Refereeing is less rigorous and papers are subjected to extensive group discussion.

Publications arising from IFIP events vary. The papers presented at the IFIP World Computer Congress and at open conferences are published as conference proceedings, while the results of the working conferences are often published as collections of selected and edited papers.

Any national society whose primary activity is in information may apply to become a full member of IFIP, although full membership is restricted to one society per country. Full members are entitled to vote at the annual General Assembly, National societies preferring a less committed involvement may apply for associate or corresponding membership. Associate members enjoy the same benefits as full members, but without voting rights. Corresponding members are not represented in IFIP bodies. Affiliated membership is open to non-national societies, and individual and honorary membership schemes are also offered.

LEARNING IN SCHOOL, HOME AND COMMUNITY

ICT for Early and Elementary Education

IFIP TC3 / WG3.5 International Working Conference on Learning with Technologies in School, Home and Community June 30–July 5, 2002, Manchester, United Kingdom

Edited by

Gail Marshall
Gail Marshall and Associates
USA

Yaacov Katz
Bar-Ilan University
Israel

KLUWER ACADEMIC PUBLISHERS
BOSTON / DORDRECHT / LONDON

Distributors for North, Central and South America:
Kluwer Academic Publishers
101 Philip Drive
Assinippi Park
Norwell, Massachusetts 02061 USA
Telephone (781) 871-6600
Fax (781) 681-9045
E-Mail <kluwer@wkap.com>

Distributors for all other countries:
Kluwer Academic Publishers Group
Post Office Box 322
3300 AH Dordrecht, THE NETHERLANDS
Telephone 31 78 6576 000
Fax 31 78 6576 254
E-Mail <services@wkap.nl>

Electronic Services <http://www.wkap.nl>

Library of Congress Cataloging-in-Publication Data

IFIP TC3/WG3.5 International Working Conference on Learning with Technologies in School, Home and Community (2002:Manchester, England)
Learning in school, home and community: ICT for early and elementary education: IFIP TC3/WG3.5 International Working Conference on Learning with Technologies in School, Home and Community, June 30–July 5, 2002, Manchester, United Kingdom / edited by Gail Marshall, Yaacov Katz.
p. cm. — (International Federation for Information Processing)
Includes bibliographical references and index.
ISBN 1-4020-7367-4
1. Early childhood education—Computer-assisted instruction—Congresses. 2. Education, Elementary—Computer-assisted instruction—Congresses. 3. Educational technology—Congresses. 4. Information technology—Congresses. I. Marshall, Gail. II. Katz, Yaacov Julian. III. IFIP Technical Committee on Education. IV. International Federation for Information Processing (Series), Working Group 3.5. V. Title.

LB1139.35.C64 I45 2003
372.133'4—dc21 2002192466

Printed on acid-free paper.
Printed in Great Britain by IBT Global, London

Contents

Preface

Manchester, one of the largest cities in the United Kingdom and a major centre of the Industrial Revolution in the 19th century, was the host city for the IFIP TC3 Working Group 3.5 (Early and Elementary Education) conference on e-learning in school, home and community. Since e-learning is a latter-day revolution, changing the way learning is designed and delivered, the conference site was an appropriate signal that the days of smoke and iron have been replaced by fibre and silicon.

Sixty-seven delegates from 14 countries, including WG 3.5 members, analysed e-learning from the perspectives of learners, teachers, evaluators and policy makers. This collection of 16 papers represents less than a third of the conference papers submitted for publication. As a refereed collection, they were chosen for the quality of presentation, the depth of their research, and the applicability of their topics and results to other educational environments around the world. Many other papers, which could not be included because of space limitations, are equally interesting, and grapple with the same problems and prospects as the papers we present to you.

The authors describe how children learn in e-settings, what interests them and how their learning often differs from adult conceptions of what the task entails. Those glimpses into e-world reality show us that childhood is a different place, one which designers of e-learning materials and environments should investigate. The descriptions of teaching and teachers' conceptions of e-learning situations show us that e-teaching is as complex as the world of the classroom has always been. Discussions of policy issues tell us that some solutions are possible and some situations are still as fraught with difficulty as they were before computers appeared in classrooms.

We have collected papers that reflect current practices and policies in all three spheres — learning, teaching and policy making — so that the reader can focus on one category or move through the volume, creating his/her own pathways through the complexity that is e-learning.

Learning

Nicola Yelland tells us that all software is not equal in children's eyes. Software evoking complex thinking is rated more highly by children than software calling for lower levels of thinking. Her work also shows us that multi-age grouping in after-school settings can be a powerful stimulus for socialisation and learning. Work by Mandy Medvin and her colleagues in a preschool and Head Start centre also shows that computer use can foster, not deter, socialisation. The team's guidance on structuring the e-learning scene for young children provides suggestions for other early and elementary school technology-based environments.

Bracha Kramarski and Adiva Liberman tell us that e-mail can fruitfully be used to scaffold the acquisition and application of mathematical skills by upper elementary school students. Matthew Pearson provides a similar window into the minds of upper elementary school students, cautioning us that the way they engage with technology differs from adult engagements and understandings.

Yaacov Katz discusses a tool for e-learning — virtual reality software — that promotes prospective nursery school teachers' understandings of the classroom from the child's point of view, a valuable learning experience for novice teachers. Ivan Kalas and Andrej Blaho describe a different learning tool. Their version of Logo, Comenius Logo, has the power to make mathematics visual, exciting and interactive — all characteristics to enhance the learners' grasp of important mathematical ideas.

Kate Crawford tells us how young learners can serve as teachers of teachers, initiating their teachers into the e-learning environment through contextually-based experiences with new technologies. She also describes how communities of learners — students, teachers, scientists and business people — can collaborate for technologically-driven change.

Teaching

While young children often adopt technology with few problems, the situation is different for teachers. Used to methods developed over years of practice, buffeted by different and often competing government directives, and challenged by the on-rush of technological innovation, teachers often believe that technology is like a fast-approaching train and they are tethered to the tracks. Steve Kennewell stresses important elements of ICT capability and then compares features of home and school settings. By suggesting goals and guidelines for monitoring progress in both settings, he helps bridge the gulf.

David Benzie provides a different perspective on the gulf, telling us that teachers are members of many different communities. They are learners, teachers and community members all at the same time. His work on the implications of power, motivation and legitimacy in those disparate roles shows us how those forces can constrain or empower.

Avril Loveless shares insights into teachers' thinking, just as Pearson showed us how children react in e-learning situations. She tells us that as practitioners in both school and community, teachers must negotiate a range of pedagogical practices as changes in technology cascade around them.

Márta Turcsányi-Szabó also discusses change but from the perspective of a teacher educator working in a country with under-developed communities in remote villages. By developing a distance learning model that includes children as active technology learners/stakeholders, her work enables us to examine how change, growth and empowerment can occur in the remote regions and in under-developed communities.

Policy

The vision of policy makers dwelling in ivory halls remote from their constituents is only partly true. Many educators involved in making or shaping policy work actively in their communities and are aware of the challenges posed by different sectors of the community. Their work attempts to inform policy at all levels — school, home and community.

Pedro Hepp and Ernesto Laval discuss the policy problems in schools and communities where conditions for technology are often inhospitable. Wind, sand and remoteness conspire to make the maintenance of technology problematic.

Sindre Røsvik also works in a rural educational setting, one which differs significantly from the Chilean situation where Hepp and Laval provide vision and support. Giske kommune in Norway, while geographically isolated, has economic and social ties with major centres of commerce and industry around the world and collaboration is a key community value.

Margaret Scanlon and David Buckingham address the publishing situation by analysing trends in e-publishing, describing resource design and development, and discussing the contentious atmosphere of policy making and implementation at the business and government level. Bridget Somekh's descriptions of four e-learning projects conducted in the UK repeat Scanlon and Buckingham's story of the multiple initiatives and mixed messages that clutter the e-learning landscape.

Margaret Cox surveys the status of e-learning evaluations and provides a framework for designing and analysing rigorous studies of the effects of e-learning on participants. Her work, developed over many years, reflects the multi-faceted approach that is essential in assessing the impact of ICT on home, school and community.

Taken as a whole, the conference papers can serve a variety of e-learning situations and inform the policies and practices of students, teachers and communities.

Gail Marshall Ph.D. has participated in the evaluation of innovative projects and practices, first at Washington University in St. Louis, MO and then at the Division of Evaluation and Research of the St. Louis Public Schools, where she was responsible for the evaluation of all federal, state and private foundation funded projects. Subsequently she joined the evaluation team for the Comprehensive School Mathematics Project (CSMP) at CEMREL, a federally funded educational research laboratory. She then rejoined the St. Louis Public Schools in 1983 as the director of the DeBalivere Project, the first system-wide initiative for ICT sponsored by local benefactors and IBM. She is also the designer of six prize-winning software programs published by Sunburst Communications and she designed workshops in conjunction with Sunburst and Apple Computers for the development of teachers' ICT expertise.

Yaacov Katz Ph.D. serves as the Chair of the Pedagogic Secretariat of the Israeli Ministry of Education. In this capacity he is responsible for strategic pedagogic and curriculum planning for the Israeli state school system. He also serves as Professor of Education at the Bar-Ilan University and heads the university's Institute for Community Education and Research.

Professor Katz specialises in the investigation of attitudes in the educational system with special emphasis on attitudes of students and teachers toward the use of ICT in learning and instruction. He has edited a number of academic volumes and published numerous scholarly articles on the above topics.

Message from the Conference Chair

For many years, IFIP's Working Group 3.5 has been providing opportunities for international scholars and educators to discuss key issues that are at the intersection of research, theory and practice. The strength of the group's work is that it brings together researchers and practitioners to exchange knowledge and discuss issues around important phenomena. It is timely for WG 3.5 to hold a conference that brings together current research, policy and practice regarding young peoples' use of computers for learning and leisure in their communities, homes and schools. Concepts such as "the digital divide" no longer apply only to rich and poor nations; they apply to the growing gaps within and between communities, and between homes and schools.

For many children access to computers in school is far less than access in their homes. Conversely, for many children, the only access they may ever have will be through their involvement in school. If we are to collectively improve the effectiveness of Information and Communication Technology to enhance young people's education we need to understand the different contexts and the implications of the differences.

The papers at the conference focused on learning with new digital technologies in a wide variety of settings. The format of the conference was especially designed to facilitate discussion and exchange of ideas around learning with ICT in those settings. By the end of the conference, we had a greater awareness and understanding of ways to harness the benefits of learning in each of the contexts to improve the overall quality of learning for young people no matter in what context they learn.

Toni Downes, Chair of the International Programme Committee

Conference Committee Members

International Programme Committee

Toni Downes, Chair, Australia
David Benzie, UK
Ivan Kalas, Slovakia
Yaacov Katz, Editor, Israel
Gail Marshall, Editor, USA
Sindre Rosvik, WG 3.5 Chair, Norway
Erling Schmidt, Denmark
Bridget Sokekh, UK
Marta Turcsanyi, Hungary

Organising Committee UK

Bridget Somekh, Chair
David Benzie
Tony Birch
Diane Mavers
Don Passey
Matthew Pearson

Manchester Metropolitan University Staff: Elaine Alkin, Tina Capewell, Jean Davidson, Adi Gal-Greenwood

Sponsors: RM, Department for Education and Skills, UK, IFIP

Part One

Learning

Learning in school and out: Formal and informal experiences with computer games in mathematical contexts

Nicola Yelland
RMIT University PO Box 71, Bundoora, Victoria, Australia, 3083; nicola.yelland@rmit.edu.au

Abstract: This paper presents the results of a study investigating the mathematical understandings, social processes and features of computer software that most appealed to children of primary school age. The study was conducted in both school and after-school contexts where computer games were used in different settings. The data reported here pertain to the out-of-school component of the study. The children attended a suburban primary school in a large urban area in Australia, and, in the after-school program located on the site, were free to choose and use the software in any way that they desired. The results of the study revealed that the children enjoyed games that had a narrative content and activities that went beyond those of traditional mathematical tasks. They preferred playing games that were problem-solving tasks, such as puzzles or spatial activities. They interacted frequently across age and gender, and indicated that they recognised the mathematical content of the majority of the games presented to them. The study highlights some major differences between in-school and after-school uses of computers, and suggests that the informal context was not only conducive to learning but also afforded opportunities for the children to interact in new and dynamic ways.

Key words: early childhood education, elementary education, social contexts, research, curriculum

1. INTRODUCTION

Computers connect us with other people, store knowledge that we can access, and provide entertainment and leisure activities for us when we are not working. Many educational justifications for the use of computers in school centre around the need to prepare students for the information age and life with computers is an integral part of that preparation.

Computer games constitute an important part of young children's lives in and out of school (Provenzo 1992), and in school contexts games are often used to consolidate practice of a specific skill such as being able to add in mathematics. Computer games also motivate students to engage conceptual material or ideas. There has been little systematic study of the use of computer games either in school or in contexts other than at-home uses of computers. After-school programmes are becoming increasingly popular as places where children go when the school day has ended and parents are working.

There have been successful examples of after-school computer clubs for students, such as the Fifth Dimension (Cole 1996) and the computer clubhouse (Resnick and Rusk 1996), as well as a variety of summer computer camps (Edwards 2002) with specific technological goals in mind. All of those contexts have demonstrated that game and design environments are conducive to the development of effective teaching and learning scenarios in which children are actively engaged with materials and ideas, promoting collaborative and individual learning.

1.1 Learning and the role of computer games in school and out

Since the early 1970's many research studies on school uses of computers have been conducted. Computer-based activities have been studied in the context of different applications, ranging from computer programming contexts, Internet-based information exchange and communication projects, community problem solving contexts through to aspects of integrating computer activities into traditional curricula. School-based use of computer games, especially in relation to mathematics, has been a recent research interest. Studies show that computer-based mathematical activities can be powerful learning tools for children (Battista and Clements 1984; Clements 1987; Yelland 1999), and the study of conceptual and skill development facilitated by mathematical computer games has become increasingly important. While information about specific environments that may promote the use and development of mathematical thinking exists, we do not know much about the role of integrating existing commercial software into mathematics programs or how the development of specific software may play a role in helping children prepare for the demands of this new century. This is an important area for research since it has been demonstrated (Upitis 1998) that students' use of video and computer games in out-of-school contexts affects their interactions with the media in school in pervasive ways. Upitis has shown that students in her study judge computer games in school contexts against the video games that they played at home, and the finding has important consequences for in-school activity since many school-based applications are less sophisticated than games, and many students find those school-based applications "boring". As a result, the students seem not to engage with the mathematical ideas inherent in the school-based applications.

Gender also plays a role in students' acceptance and use of software. The E GEMS project found significant differences in performance based on gender (Inkpen, Klawe, Lawry, Sedighian, Leroux and Hsu 1994). The research also indicates that the role of the teacher was critical in explicating the mathematical inferences in games. In a related study, De Jean, Upitis, Koch, and Young (1999) also noted the importance of a teacher or mentor who could help children to make connections with the mathematics content in the computer games that they played. They stated, "Without specific guidance from a teacher or mentor, it would appear that many students, and significantly more girls than boys ... will not detect the underlying mathematical concepts that might be embedded within a computer game" (216). Other research has also highlighted the importance of the teacher in making mathematical connections explicit to learners (Leitze 1997).

It is apparent that computer games have the potential to engage children in learning in ways that were not possible without them. Game contexts motivate children to play with ideas, interact and collaborate with peers in sharing strategies and articulating ideas. Through their work with the games, they acquire skills for learning and new knowledge that seem to be adaptive to new and differing contexts. The ways in which children do this is still not clearly understood and the present study sought to add to our knowledge by identifying the levels of interest, mathematical understandings and learning of students as they engaged with computer games in an after-school context.

2. THE STUDY

The study was designed to examine and describe the ways in which children in after-care settings chose, used and evaluated computer software designed to develop specific mathematical processes and thinking. It was especially concerned with obtaining data that would elucidate:

- mathematical learning via descriptions of the mathematical understandings that emerged as children played and interacted in computer-based contexts, and the ways in which children developed and refined their mathematical strategies and representations as they gained experience with the various types of software;

- social processes by examining the ways in which the design and content of the software influenced social interactions during play; and by examining if the interactions moderated how the children viewed the software. Of particular interest here were constructions of gender which may be influential since computer games have been noted as being more appealing to boys than girls (Cassell and Jenkins 1998).

We were also interested in the features of computer software design that appealed to children, especially features that initially attracted them to a game and those which had a sustaining effect. Additionally, we thought it was important to consider how teachers and children selected software for use, and the ways in which they made sense of the various characteristics inherent in the different games.

2.1 Subjects

Twenty children attending a suburban after-school care programme participated in the study. They ranged in age from 5 years, 6 months to 10 years, 6 months and spanned all seven grades of the primary school years. The children played the games on two laptop computers that were adjacent to other activities in the hall where the program was located. One laptop was attached to a multi-gen recorder that recorded computer images to video-tape and that was digitally mixed with input from a camera focussed on the users of the software.

The research assistant observed children on the other computer and made detailed field notes related to the three aims of the study. Profiles of each child were then created and based on the videotaped and field observation data. The children were interviewed before the study commenced about their experience with computers and computer activities in home and school contexts. When the study was completed they were interviewed for a second time to ascertain their favourite programs, what they particularly liked about those programs, and what they most liked about playing the games in the after-school context.

3. RESULTS

3.1 Children's game preferences

Twenty-five games, all with mathematical content, were available and no restrictions were placed on their use. It was immediately evident that three games were the most popular as evidenced by their almost continuous use:

The Logical Journey of the Zoombinis, Counting on Frank and Carmen San Diego (mathematics).

Some of the young children found it difficult to articulate the reasons why they liked the games and mainly gave answers such as: "Don't know," or "It was fun!" The older children were able to focus on specific aspects of the game that they enjoyed. For example, Divy (Year 7) said he liked the Zoombinis software, " ... because you can go through the levels and sometimes like showed some things - the levels were good. It's fun to play and you can choose your Zoombinis - make them how you want." Similarly, Kyle (Year 7) said, "Zoombinis, because I like adventure games more than other types and like inventing Zoombinis." Hannah (Year 3) said, "Zoombinis and Madeline. I just like them. Good pictures and interesting things to do."

3.1.1 Specific features appealing to children

Overall, three features of games seemed to make them popular with the children:

- the format of the games: Puzzles were more attractive than simple (e.g., addition) activities that were an end in themselves or resulted in a reward or trinket for effort expended.

  Maddy (Year 1) said she liked Secret Paths "... because you find stones.... I like the girls and like what they made out of the computer... I liked when they told us about their Mums and friends said and the pictures... I likes the pathways pictures."

- The design element combined with a narrative: The children in the study enjoyed making their own characters (e.g., Zoombinis) and chose as their three favourite games ones which were set in a story context.

  For example, Kyle said, "My favourite is Zoombinis.... Because I like adventure games more than other types and I like inventing Zoombinis...". The children became very possessive about their Zoombinis and made comments like "Don't you dare hurt my Zoombinis," (Richard Year 4) when the troll in one of the puzzles "threatened" his creations. Players also engaged in conversation with the characters as they were playing. Richard said, "Ok, we push on. Come on you guys you have to come with us.... I saved your lives guys so you should be thanking me. I did quite a lot of work for you."

- software that catered for a variety of levels of interest and ability: This was evident in Zoombinis, when Marcus indicated that Zoombinis was his favourite because "... you can go on different levels" but also in games like Math Workshop which had three different levels when Divy (Year 7) said it was only "Ok", because he "...could change the levels and watch the gorilla knock the pins down!"

3.2 Mathematical understandings

The data revealed that for the younger children, those up to Year 4, mathematics was mainly related to numbers and "sums". The older children, especially those in Year 6 and 7 recognised that the Zoombinis software was mathematics because it had "puzzles" and "combinations". In fact one of the things that appealed to children in the older age group about games like Zoombinis was that the mathematics was "cool maths, really hard maths" (Kyle, Year 7). In contrast, Kyle noted that Math Workshop was maths too but "... it was really easy, boring maths." Kyle also thought that he had learned "new maths stuff" by playing Zoombinis because of the different levels. The younger children did not seem to recognise the shape activities (e.g., in James Discovers Math) as mathematics. Maddy (Year 1) said she liked the Shapes game in James and when asked if it was maths she said, "No, it's matching pictures."

Of interest here was not only the difference across the age range but also the fact that the older children seemed to enjoy being challenged in the games whereas the younger group just wanted to play the games in "easy" mode for "fun". At the same time they enjoyed Zoombinis which was always challenging to all the children who played it and *all* the children played it.

One afternoon in the third week Maddy (Year 1) was offering advice to Kevin (Year 5) about how to get the Zoombinis across the bridge in the first activity based on finding their similar attributes. It was Kevin's first time with the program and Maddy had already had experience and success with the game and could advise him! This would not have been possible in school contexts and provided Maddy with the opportunity to feel good about the fact that she could make a contribution to the successful experience of an older student.

3.3 Interactions

The nature and extent of the interactions while the children were playing the computer games were interesting and complex. There were a number of factors which influenced the ways in which the children interacted:

- the environment: Free choice and after-school context;

- the software design: Puzzle/narrative context vs. activity-based separate activities;
- the age and gender of the children.

The after-school environment was very conducive for interactions and collaborations. No restrictions were placed on the children in terms of what they could play, unless someone else was using it and we only had to introduce time restrictions after the first three weeks when the children claimed that some were "hogging" the computer time. The physical space helped as well. The laptop computers were placed on large tables and children could sit beside one another and bring chairs along to perch on. This still meant that one, perhaps two, children had the main roles but the space allowed for up to six other children to be involved in the experience, a stark contrast to school use of the games where a maximum of two is usually the norm.

The context was also more conducive to extended use of the games, which tend to have time restrictions placed on them in school classrooms where short games without a narrative are the norm. Such games can be played and repeated for practice in short allocations of time to allow for everyone to have a turn. However with software such as Zoombinis, Counting on Frank and Carmen San Diego it is useful to have longer periods of time for playing, since, in the short term, gains are small. Additionally, the activity-based software packages, that is those which are composed of separate activities usually around a theme or character, are more easily accommodated in maths curricula since they focus on traditional concept areas such as number, measurement, and space whereas games such as Zoombinis focus more on problem solving and reasoning skills.

Games such as Zoombinis, Counting on Frank and Carmen San Diego all afforded opportunities to share strategies and collaborate since they contained problem-solving activities. It is more difficult to interact when you are being asked to add 6 and 7 or multiply numbers. The same can be said for copying shapes to a new picture. In this way, those software programs which were "not simple maths" (Matthias, Year 3), were characterised by much higher levels of interactions than those which had a number of short and simple games.

It was also apparent that programs like Zoombinis, Counting on Frank and Carmen San Diego were liked by both boys and girls, but that other games were favoured by one or the other of the genders. For example, Madeline was preferred by girls only while boys, especially the younger ones (year 1 and 2), really enjoyed Land Before Time as dinosaurs seem to have a wide appeal that is mainly related to boys.

The nature and extent of interactions was mapped for each child and showed considerable variation that seemed to be individualised for all 20 children. Some children we tended to characterise as *watchers* rather than *doers*. They might offer advice on some occasion to a peer and then would use a game by themselves on one occasion while on another occasion they might be part of a large team of players determined to find the last jelly bean giving them the solution to the Counting on Frank puzzle. To show the nature and extent of the variety of style of interactions two are presented as Figures 1 and 2.

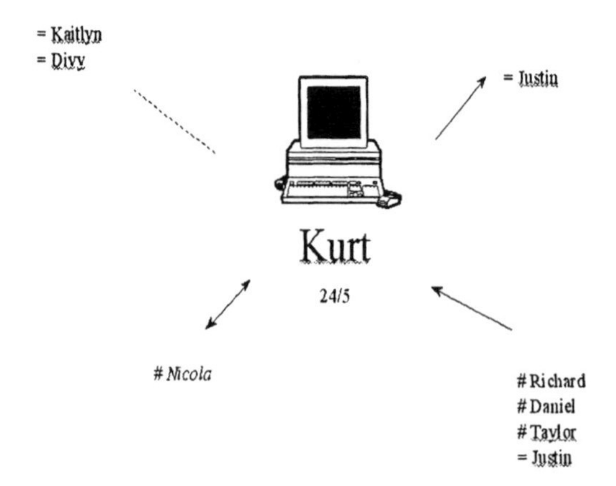

Figure 1. Interactions with Kurt

Figure 1 maps the interactions with Kurt on May 24 in week 3 of the project. It reveals that when Kurt (Year 4) was playing Zoombinis over a period of 48 minutes three peers, Richard (Year 4), Daniel (Year 5) and Taylor (Year 3), spent more than two minutes interacting with him by asking and responding to questions and making general comments about the game. Justin (Year 7) came to join the group for less than two minutes when Kurt asked him a question about strategy and Kaitlyn (Year 1) and Divy (Year 7) stood and watched for a short time (less than two minutes). The researcher (Nicola) engaged Kurt in conversation about what he and his peers were doing while they were playing the game and Kurt was on the keyboard. The type of map was a stark contrast to those for games such as Jumpstart or Math Workshop where there was little or no interaction.

Figure 2 shows all the people that Maddy interacted with over six sessions in May. While Maddy was on the computer playing games she both asked for advice and interacted with respondents. She also listened to advice from others without reacting verbally to them. There was no preferential style in this respect. Additionally, the range of peers that Maddy interacted with spanned all year and age levels. Only two children (Hannah and Marcus) watched Maddy without offering comments or asking questions. The timing of the interactions varied from whole sessions, shown by the asterisk, to less than two minutes (shown with =), to more than two minutes (#), but not the whole session.

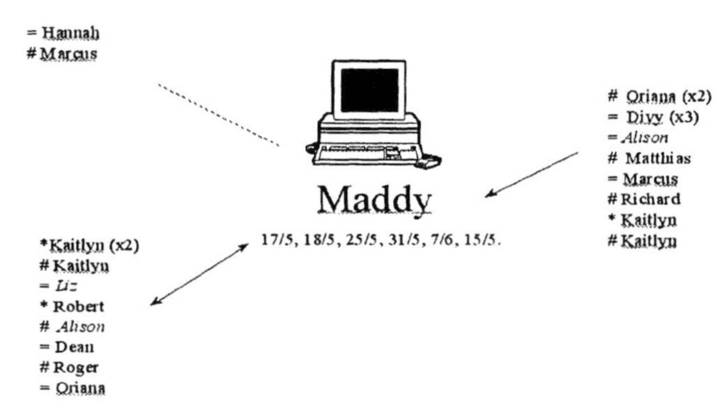

Figure 2. Maddy's interactions around computer games

We noted that the interactions were very unpredictable and the nature of the after-school program was such that one rarely saw no interactions, in direct contrast to data being collected at the current time with the same games in a classroom-based study.

4. CONCLUSIONS

The study has provided new information about the appeal of mathematical computer games in an after-school context and has revealed that children love to play computer games, especially open-ended puzzles or problem-solving games as opposed to repetitious skill reinforcement/ practice games. The results from the study have shown that well-designed computer games not only act as a stimulus for learning and engagement with mathematical ideas and processes, but afford the opportunity for children to participate in collaborative problem solving in new and dynamic ways. The study has highlighted differences between in-school and out-of-school learning opportunities which may inform teachers and carers in both settings. Overall, it would seem that the after-school environment provided a valuable context for exploring mathematical concepts with technology and that one of the most pleasing aspects was the interaction of children across age groups, not usually possible within school settings.

REFERENCES

Battista, M. and Clements, D.H. (1984) A case for a Logo-based elementary school geometry curriculum. *Arithmetic Teacher* 36 11-17.

Cassell, J. and Jenkins, H. (1998) *From Barbie to Mortal Kombat.* Cambridge: MIT Press.

Clements, D.H. (1987) Longitudinal study of the effects of Logo programming on cognitive abilities and achievement. *Journal of Educational Computing Research* 3 73-94.

Cole, M. (1996) *Cultural Psychology*. Cambridge, MA: Harvard University Press.

De Jean, J., Upitis, R., Koch, C., and Young, J. (1999) The story of Phoenix Quest: How girls respond to a prototype language and mathematics computer game. *Gender and Education* 11 2 207–223.

Edwards, L. (2002) Learning by design: Environments that support girls' learning with technology. In N. Yelland and A. Rubin (eds.). *Ghost in the Machine: Women's Voices in Research with Technology.* New York: Peter Lang.

Inkpen, K., Klawe, M., Lawry, L., Sedighian, K., Leroux, S. and Hsu, D. (1994) "We have never-forgetful flowers in our garden": Girls' responses to electronic games. *Journal of Computers in Mathematics and Science Teaching* 13 4 383–403.

Leitze, A.R. (1997) Connecting process problem solving to children's literature. *Teaching Children Mathematics* 3 74–77.

Provenzo, E. F. (1992) The video generation. *American School Board Journal* 179 3 29-32.

Resnick, M. and Rusk, N. (1996) The computer clubhouse: Preparing for life in a digital world. *IBM Systems Journal* 35 3 431-439.

Upitis, R. (1998). From hackers to luddites, game players to game creators: Profiles of adolescent students using technology. *Journal of Curriculum Studies* 30 3 293–318.

Yelland, N.J. (1999) Reconceptualising schooling with technology. *Information Technology in Childhood Education* 1 1 39-59.

BIOGRAPHY

Nicola Yelland is Professor and Head of the Department of School and Early Childhood Education at the RMIT University in Melbourne. Nicola's research over the last decade has investigated the ways in which children learn with new information technologies in school and in out-of-school contexts. She is the author of *Early Mathematical Explorations* with Carmel Diezmann and Deborah Butler, and has edited three other books, *Gender in Early Childhood* (Routledge), *Innovations in Practice* (NAEYC) and *Ghosts in the Machine: Women's Voices in Research with Technology*. Nicola works with teachers exploring the ways in which ICT can be incorporated into learning contexts to make them more interesting and motivating for children. She has worked both in Australia and overseas to encourage rethinking curricula in the information age.

Using technology to encourage social problem solving in preschoolers

Mandy B. Medvin, Diana Reed, Deborah Behr and Elizabeth Spargo
Westminster College, New Wilmington, PA 16172-0001, US; CDI Head Start Serving Lawrence County, 301 E. Long Ave., New Castle, PA 16101 medvinm@westminster.edu; reedd@westminster.edu; behrd@westminster.edu

Abstract: A recent emphasis in the early childhood literature has been on using computers to facilitate social skills in preschool children. Findings are mixed on how well children collaborate when using computers. This inconsistency indicates that the design of the computer curriculum may dictate the nature of the climate of use.

Our work examines a cooperative classroom approach to computer use to "alter" the roles of students and teachers. Our premise is that computers can encourage socialization among children, thereby forming the basis for early cooperative learning.

Key words: collaboration, teacher education, early childhood education, social contexts

1. INTRODUCTION

Do computers isolate? Or do they encourage interaction among preschool children? Some research shows that children enjoy working with one another on the computer by making suggestions, playing games together, and providing assistance (Davidson 1989; Shade, Nida, Lipinski, and Watson 1986; Muller and Perlmutter 1985). Other studies find that children are aggressive in obtaining access to the computer, and that the play is competitive rather than cooperative (Anderson 1998). Our premise is that the design of the classroom environment can encourage either isolation or integration. The goal of our project was to make the computer a "social center" in our classroom, and to test our approach by extending it across two very different preschool settings: A university preschool laboratory and a specially designed Head Start preschool for disadvantaged children.

We chose this approach for several reasons. First, our school emphasizes a Vygotskian approach to learning with peer interaction as a means of promoting social and cognitive development. According to Vygotsky (1978), "... human learning presupposes a specific social nature and a process by which children grow into the intellectual life of those around them..." (88). We do not separate social and cognitive functions but examine them together as a framework for learning. We are also inspired by socio-cultural models of cognition, where children attain learning goals via scaffolding (Greenfield 1984; Woods and Woods 1996) or "guided participation" by adults or peers (Rogoff 1990; 1995).

Second, many studies indicate that preschool is an important time for the development of peer relations, which in turn form the cornerstone for children's later life success (Parker and Asher 1987). For example, children who play cooperatively in preschool and transition to kindergarten with a familiar peer have an easier time adjusting to school (Ladd and Price 1987). Our idea is that the skills that predicate higher social success in preschool can be enhanced by participation in collaborative tasks.

Finally, since many children consider computers exciting and fun (McBride and Austin 1986), we theorised that the computer station might provide a common focus for less social children to be involved in the classroom social network. Our own anecdotal observations of what occurs in our school when children gather together around the computer are reflected in this paper.

2. PEER COLLABORATION IN YOUNG CHILDREN: RESEARCH PERSEPCTIVES

A large body of research supports the idea that peer collaboration can lead to advances in cognitive understanding given the appropriate design of tasks and scaffolding on the part of the teacher. The majority of studies have focused on carefully designed laboratory experiments which pair peers on a type of collaborative task rather than examining natural interactions in the classroom. Findings from the research, however, may be helpful in thinking about setting up a facilitative classroom environment.

Factors that influence preschool peer collaboration include age, expertise, and type of task. Cooper (1980) demonstrated that older children were more successful than younger preschoolers on a matching task due to higher levels of on-topic conversational directives. Azmitia (1988) showed that same-age novices working with an expert improved more than novices working alone or in pairs on a Lego model task. Holmes (1997) found a greater exchange of information on a more complex model task than a single bead task. In addition, girls who used reasoning on complex tasks had higher task success than those who did not, while boys who used reasoning had greater success on a simpler bead task. The overall findings indicate that preschool children can collaborate successfully and show improved task performance in pairs versus working individually. Therefore, it is worthwhile to explore the use of collaboration when working on computers in the preschool classroom.

3. OUR COLLABORATION

To ensure a variety of ideas and mutual involvement in the project, a series of meetings were conducted at different points during the project between Head Start and the Westminster College laboratory preschool staff. Our initial intervention focused on a classroom of eighteen 4 and 5 year olds at the laboratory preschool, and two classrooms of eighteen 3 to 5 year olds each at the Head Start site. Video cameras were placed in each school to document children's interactions at the computer and the same programs were used at both sites. In addition, we received a National Association for the Education of Young Children (NAEYC) Membership Action Grant to develop a teacher training workshop for daycare and preschools in our area.

3.1 Experiences at the lab preschool: Our initial site

The Westminster College laboratory preschool, located in rural western Pennsylvania, serves a relatively middle-class population from the surrounding area. Many of our families have a computer at home. Prior to the intervention, preschool volunteers took children out of the classroom to work individually with the computers in a nearby computer lab.

We purchased a computer and moved it into the preschool classroom. To facilitate social interactions, we placed it in an area that was convenient but not too busy (Davis and Shade 1994), and put several chairs at the center so children could work together. We used several activities to acquaint children with computers and the programs, so they could more easily assist one another at our centre. A guest speaker introduced the computer and opened it up so we could look inside. Children played directional games using a large cardboard "mouse" and participated in "fun" art activities, such as painting using old floppy as well as creating computer wire art. Finally, we familiarized small groups of students with several computer games from Millie's Math House (Edmark 1992), which we then used at our center.

3.2 Facilitating cooperative use of computers

We introduced three rules to encourage social usage, sharing, and helping behavior at the computer — Find a Friend, Help a Friend, and Share the Mouse — to facilitate children's social problem solving in order that "individual skills originate in cooperative activity through a scaffolding process" (Greenfield 1984). The Find a Friend rule means that two or more children must be playing at the computer at all times. Help a Friend encourages children to stay and help the child with the mouse, play the computer program by providing directions and information, by pointing, and by physically helping to guide the mouse. Share the Mouse prompts children to pass the mouse to the friend next to them after they have played for a while. Children are encouraged to "use their words" and switch chairs to help with taking turns. We also took pictures of students engaged in the three activities and posted the rules by the computer as a reminder.

Children immediately seemed to enjoy working at the computer together though they needed some assistance to follow the rules. Initially, a teacher stayed at the center to help them, and to encourage them to work out conflicts and provide support. For example, if a child asked the teacher for help in changing the computer game, the teacher might say, "I know Jennie has played that game before. If you ask her, I'm sure she'll tell you where to click the mouse to change the game." The teacher also encouraged children to point to the picture prompts and remind their friends of the rules.

As the children needed less guidance the teachers gradually spent less time at the computer. Woods and Woods (1996) said that "... effective guidance involves the transfer of responsibility from (teacher) to learner." The computer became a peer-led center. Children spontaneously offered assistance to their friends in changing the game and exploring the programs. The children helped each other play new games as well. Some students had the same games at home and were able to assist their peers. At other times they simply problem solved until they found the solution.

Sharing was a difficult task and was often mediated by the teacher. The children, however, developed their own strategies for deciding who went next. Eventually, we introduced a timer to assist children in deciding when it was someone else's turn, which worked well. This approach was so successful that we next examined this model at the Head Start site.

3.3 Reactions from the Head Start site

The Villa Maria Head Start program, located in the same county as the laboratory preschool, serves children from low-income families in the surrounding rural area. At least ten percent of the children have special needs and often that percentage is higher. Few of the children had access to computers prior to entering our program. Our goal was the same as the preschool lab — to change the computer station to a more cooperative centre.

Our strategies to encourage social interaction were different from the laboratory preschool since we thought the Head Start children would benefit by a more structured approach. To facilitate sharing, we used a sign-up sheet to let children know when it was their turn. We placed the children in small groups of three or four, and strategically matched quiet children with more talkative ones to promote language use. Often children not on the list would join the sessions until a crowd formed around the computer.

We found that the larger group sizes resulted in more socialisation and mediation taking place at the computer without the potential problems that we had imagined might occur, such as impatience while waiting turns with the mouse and a short attention span if the child wasn't actually manipulating the mouse. Children were very engaged, offering suggestions to the computer user, and they often learned the program by watching the game being played. By helping the user, the waiting children felt a part of the process, which made the wait more tolerable and helped increase the children's patience.

We also found that the computer provided a positive outlet for the more dominant personalities in our classroom. Children used their natural leadership abilities and temperament in a positive manner that was well accepted by peers. Also, the group work provided a great opportunity for children who were usually passive to develop leadership skills by instructing others on the computer. Children helped peers who were younger or had motor difficulties in moving the mouse.

Almost half of the children were receiving speech and language therapy. Working at the computer with peers seemed to provide a common focus that encouraged social interaction and language use. For example, in one session Joan spent most of the time silently sitting on the facilitator's lap while watching the screen. Then, after taking a turn at the mouse with the assistance of Steve and Alfonse, she helped a younger child move the mouse and verbally "figure out" the program. At the laboratory school we found that one child with language delays taught other children how to use a game he had at home.

Overall, we found that children "took over" the computer station at both sites with some guidance thus employing a peer collaborative model. Other studies report similar findings and indicate that the computer may foster more interaction than other areas of the preschool classroom (Muhlstein and Croft 1986; Muller and Perlmutter 1985).

4. ACCOMPLISHMENTS AT BOTH SITES

What were the major accomplishments of the children and why did they happen? In addition, how did the differences in techniques between the two sites influence outcomes?

Over time, the accomplishments at both sites were similar for the children, regardless of differences in background or experience with computers: (1) initially students offered to help and seemed to enjoy the idea of helping others at the computer; (2) children using the mouse learned after some practice to ask their peers for help if they needed it and refused assistance less often over time; they began to collaborate with their peers, and the help offered was more appropriate to the task at hand; (3) sharing required more facilitation by teachers than helping, though teacher facilitation gradually decreased; still, over half the time children settled sharing issues without the help of the teacher; (4) new friendships were formed as children who did not normally play together realised each other's strengths and competencies.

We believe that there were several causal agents making this approach successful: (1) the approach fit our current philosophy of facilitating cognitive development in a social context and was an extension of goals at other centres; (2) teachers already have experience facilitating social skills and so this approach built on already existing abilities; (3) we continued to monitor the computer groups to help enhance children's skills; (4) children are highly motivated to work on the computer and thus will be more interested to fill required roles in order to play. In essence, to obtain access to the computer, they must be social.

5. CONCLUSION

Researchers have questioned the use of computers in the preschool classroom, indicating that high levels of adult assistance are needed, child control is decreased, play is diminished and peers become isolated (Henninger 1994). Our results indicate that with some initial facilitation it is the children who "run" the computer center, becoming experts in using the programs, collaborating and assisting each other. Teachers were comfortable with this approach, as it affirmed their models for how preschool classrooms should operate. Thus computers, when used appropriately, have the potential to facilitate the development of important social skills needed for entry into kindergarten. We also feel strongly that it is not how many computers you have but what you do with them that makes the difference in the preschool classroom.

REFERENCES

Anderson, G. T. (1998) Comparison of the types of cooperative problem-solving behaviors in four learning centers. Poster presentation at Head Start's Fourth National Research Conference. Washington, D.C.

Azmitia, M. (1988) Peer interaction and problem solving: When are two heads better than one? *Child Development* 59 87-96.

Cooper, C. R. (1980) Development of collaborative problem solving among preschool children. *Developmental Psychology* 16 5 433-440.

Davidson, J. (1989) *Children and Computers Together in the Early Childhood Classroom.* New York: Delmar.

Davis, B. C. and Shade, D. D. (1994) Integrate, don't isolate! Computers in the early childhood curriculum. *ERIC Digest* (December). No. EDO-PS-94-17.

Greenfield, P. M. (1984) A theory of the teacher in the learning activities of everyday life. In B. Rogoff and J. Lave (eds.) *Everyday Cognition: Its Development in Social Context* Cambridge: Harvard University Press 117-138.

Henniger, M. L. (1994) Computers and preschool children's play: Are they compatible? *Journal of Computing in Childhood Education* 5 3 231-239.

Holmes, H. A. (1997, April) Preschool children's collaborative problem-solving interactions: Influence of task, partner gender, and conversational style. Poster presentation at the biennial meeting of the Society for Research in Child Development. Washington, D.C.

Ladd, G. W. and Price, J. M. (1987) Predicting children's social and school adjustment following the transition from preschool to kindergarten. *Child Development* 58 1168-1189.

McBride, K. J. and Austin, A. M. (1986) Computer affect of preschool children and perceived affect of their parents, teachers, and peers. *The Journal of Genetic Psychology* 147 4 497-506.

Millie's Math House. (1992) Redmond, WA: Edmark Corporation.

Muller, A. A. and Perlmutter, M. (1985) Preschool children's problem-solving interactions at computers and jigsaw puzzles. *Journal of Applied Developmental Psychology* 6 173-186.

Muhlstein, E. A. and Croft, D. J. (1986) Using the microcomputer to enhance language experiences and the development of cooperative play among preschool children. Cupertino, CA: De Anza College. ERIC Document Reproduction Service No. ED269 004.

Parker, J. D. and Asher, S. R. (1987) Peer relations and later personal adjustment: Are low-accepted children at risk? *Psychological Bulletin* 102 3 357-389.

Rogoff, B. (1990) *Apprenticeship in Thinking: Cognitive Development in Social Context.* New York: Oxford University Press.

Rogoff, B. (1995) Observing sociocultural activity on three planes: Participatory appropriation, guided participation, and apprenticeship. In J.V. Wertsch, P. del Rio, and A. Alvarez (eds.) *Sociocultural Studies of Mind.* New York: Cambridge University Press.

Shade, D. D., Nida, R. E., Lipinski, J. M. and Watson, J. A. (1986) Microcomputers and preschoolers: Working together in a classroom setting. *Computers in the School* 3 2 53-61.

Tharp, R. G. and Gallimore, R. (1991) *Rousing Minds to Life: Teaching, Learning, and Schooling in Social Context.* New York: Cambridge University Press.

Woods, D. and Woods, H. (1996) Vygotsky, tutoring and learning. *Oxford Review of Education* 22 1 5-16.

Vygotsky, L. S. (1978) *Mind in Society.* Cambridge, MA: Harvard University Press.

BIOGRAPHIES

Mandy Medvin is an associate professor of Psychology at Westminster College in New Wilmington, PA, and director of the Preschool Lab program. She has presented at workshops and conferences on the social use of computers.

Diana Reed is headteacher and Deborah Behr is a teacher at the Westminster College Preschool Lab. They regularly present at workshops on encouraging social development in young children.

Elizabeth Spargo is educational director of CDI Head Start serving Lawrence County and is a regular presenter at workshops.

Using electronic mail communication and metacognitive instruction to improve mathematical problem solving

Bracha Kramarski and Adiva Liberman
School of Education, Bar-Ilan University, Ramat-Gan 52900, Israel; kramarb@mail.biu.ac.il

Abstract: The present study investigated the effects of e-mail communication between teachers and students embedded within metacognitive instruction on mathematical problem solving. Three learning environments are compared: (a) e-mail communication with metacognitive instruction (META+EMAIL); (b) e-mail communication without metacognitive instruction (EMAIL); and (c) face-to-face communication (CONT group).

Participants were 119 fifth-grade students (boys and girls), who practiced six weeks of problem solving on authentic tasks in three classes. Students who were exposed to e-mail conversation and metacognitive instruction (EMAIL+META) outperformed students who were not exposed to metacognitive instruction (EMAIL and CONT) on problem solving. The effects were observed on various aspects of solving authentic tasks: (a) processing information; (b) using mathematical strategies; and (c) using mathematical communcation. The EMAIL students outperformed the CONT students only on one criterion: Using mathematical strategies.

Key words: elementary education, conditions for learning, research, networks

1. INTRODUCTION

Interest in communication is both more widespread and more central to mathematics education reform efforts than ever before. The National Council of Teachers of Mathematics (2000) emphasises the importance of problem solving and communicating mathematical ideas, not simply providing isolated answers. The new reforms for teaching of mathematics redirect teachers to focus on problem solving within authentic contexts. From a motivational perspective, such tasks are challenging and relevant to the students' world and daily life (OECD 2000). Although authentic tasks are important, little is known at present about how to enhance students' ability to solve such tasks. The question, "What characteristics should a learning environment have to facilitate the construction of students' ability to solve authentic problems?" merits further research.

1.1 Using electronic mail communication and metacognitive instruction

One of the most immediate communication benefits networked computers offer is electronic mail. E-mail has the potential for becoming a near-universal source of communication within the next decades (Deaudelin and Richer 1999). It allows asynchronous exchanges and permits one-to-one as well as one-to-many communications. Of the two, teachers should take advantage of one-to-one communication because it makes up for the lack of student-teacher interpersonal communication, inevitable in the classroom context. It may be an important tool for providing individual support to students. However, that particular technology, as has been the case with prior technologies, raises the question about pedagogical approaches.

A review of pedagogical approaches shows that the majority emphasise the development of metacognition or learning-to-learn abilities. Many researchers (e.g., Butler and Winne 1995; Mevarech and Kramarski 1997) maintain that learning-to-learn abilities proved to be essential to the improvement of learning performances and problem solving. Butler and Winne (1995) describe Self Regulation Learning (SRL) as a style of activities for problem solving that includes: Evaluating goals, thinking of strategies and choosing the most appropriate strategy for solving the problem. The IMPROVE method (Mevarech and Kramarski 1997) emphasises the importance of providing each student with the opportunity to construct mathematical meaning by involving him/her in mathematical learning via the use of self questioning that focuses on: (a) comprehending the problem ("What is the problem all about"?); (b) constructing connections between previous and new knowledge ("What are the similarities/differences between the problem at hand and the problems you have solved in the past? and why?"); (c) use of strategies appropriate for solving the problem ("What are the strategies/tactics/principles appropriate for solving the problem and why?"); and in some studies also (d) reflecting on the processes and the solution ("What did I do wrong here?"; "Does the solution make sense?").

Generally speaking, researchers (e.g., Schoenfeld 1992; Mevarech and Kramarski 1997; Kramarski, Liberman, and Mevarech 2001) reported positive effects of metacognitive instruction on students' mathematical achievement. There is also evidence showing that the effects of metacognitive feedback in a computerised environment were more positive than the effects of result feedback on mathematical reasoning (Kramarski and Zeichner 2001). So we hypothesised that providing metacognitive instruction embedded in e-mail communication would exert more positive effects on students' problem solving than using e-mail communication, which in turn would exert more positive effects than face-to-face communication without metacognitive instruction.

2. METHOD

Participants, 119 fifth-grade students (boys and girls, mean age 10.4), practiced six weeks of problem solving in three classes. The EMAIL+META group (n=40) was exposed to e-mail communication embedded with metacognitive instruction and the EMAIL class (n=40) was exposed to e-mail communication without metacognitive instruction. The CONT class (n=39) was exposed to face-to-face communication without metacognitive instruction and served as a control group.

2.1 Treatments

Students in all conditions practiced problem solving of three authentic tasks for four weeks (90 minutes a week) and they were asked to reflect by writing their decisions during the problem-solving process. The following is an example of such an authentic task:

> The Hall Task: You have to arrange a Hall for a party in school. Here are three different price proposals for renting the Hall: The price is NIS 1,000 for renting the Hall, no matter how many people will arrive. The basic price for renting the Hall is NIS 400. But, if the number of participants will be more than 200, you have to pay NIS 3 more for each person. The basic price for renting the Hall is NIS 200 and in addition you have to pay NIS 3 for each participant. Decide which offer is most worthwhile. Explain your reasoning.
>
> A full accurate answer regards correctly organizing the information by using tables, diagrams or algebraic expressions, making a correct suggestion based on the given information and providing verbal explanations to justify the suggestion.

The study was implemented in pairs, as follows: Each student, in turn, read the task aloud, tried to solve it and explained his/her mathematical reasoning. Whenever there was no consensus, the students discussed the issue until the disagreement was resolved. Students were encouraged to talk about the task, explain it to each other, and approach it from different perspectives.

2.1.1 E-mail communication

The students who were exposed to EMAIL communication practiced problem solving authentic tasks once a week in the computer lab (90 minutes). They were encouraged to communicate with their teacher, who was called the "virtual teacher". They practised how to send/receive assignments and submit questions regarding the solution process, and how to send/open attachment files. They were also encouraged to ask the teacher for help when they encountered difficulties in understanding and correcting the solution, if needed, after receiving feedback by EMAIL from the teacher.

2.1.1.1 Metacognitive instruction

The metacognitive instruction was based on Mevarech's and Kramarski's (1997) IMPROVE technique. The method used four self-addressed metacognitive questions:

- Comprehension questions were designed to prompt students to reflect on the problem/task before solving it. In addressing a comprehension question, students had to read the problem/task aloud and describe the task in their own words. They tried to understand what the tasks/concepts mean and answered questions such as, "What is the problem/task all about?"; "What is the question?"; "What are the meanings of the mathematical concepts?"
- Connection questions were designed to prompt students to focus on similarities and differences between the problem/task they work on and the problem/task or set of problems/tasks that they had already solved such as, "How is this problem/task different from/similar to what you have already solved? Explain why."
- Strategic questions were designed to prompt students to consider which strategies are appropriate for solving the given problem/task and for what reasons. So students had to describe what strategy/tactic/ principle can be used in order to solve the problem/task, why the strategy/tactic/principle is most appropriate for solving the problem/task, and how to organize the information to solve the problem/task.

– Reflection questions were designed to prompt students on their understanding and feelings during the solution process ("What am I doing?"; "Does it make sense?"; "What difficulties/feelings I face in solving the task?"; "How can I verify the solution?"; "Can I use another approach for solving the task?").

Students used the metacognitive questions during their discourse in small group activities and in their written explanations when they solved the mathematical tasks. Teachers modelled the use of the metacognitive questions in their introductions, reviews and when they provided help. Students also studied according to the IMPROVE method and EMAIL communication described above, and were encouraged to use the metacognitive questions — comprehension, connection, strategic and reflection — in their communication with the "virtual teacher". The teachers used the metacognitive questions when they provided help in their e-mail messages.

2.1.2 EMAIL condition

Students in that class studied the same way as students in the EMAIL+META class but they were not exposed to the metacognitive instruction.

2.1.3 Control condition

Students studied the same way as students under the EMAIL+META and EMAIL conditions but they were not exposed to e-mail communication nor to metacognitive instruction. Students were asked to submit the solution of the authentic tasks in writing and to reflect on their solution process.

3. MEASURES

Two measures were used to assess students' mathematical problem solving: (a) a pre-test that focused on students' mathematical knowledge prior to the beginning of the study and (b) a post-test that assessed students' ability to solve authentic mathematical problems.

The 22-item multiple-choice item pre-test of basic factual knowledge and open-ended computation problems was administered to all students at the beginning of the school year and covered arithmetic knowledge taught prior to the beginning of the study. The following content appeared on the test: Whole numbers, fractions, decimals and percents. For each item students received a score of either 1 (correct answer) or 0 (incorrect answer), and a total score ranging from 0 to 22 (Kuder Richardson reliability coefficient was =.87).

The post-test consisted of an authentic task to assess students' ability to solve such tasks as shown in Figure 1.

> Your classmates organize a party. The school will provide the soft drinks, and you are asked to order the pizza. The class budget is NIS 85.00. Of course, you want to order as many pizzas as you can. Here are proposals of three local pizza restaurants and their prices. Compare the prices and suggest the cheapest offer to the class treasurer. Write a report to the class treasurer in which you justify your suggestion.

TYPE OF PIZZA	PRICE PER PIZZA	DIAMETER	PRICE FOR SUPPLEMENTS
	PIZZA BOOM		
PERSONAL PIZZA	3.50 N.I.S	15	4.00 N.I.S
SMALL	6.50 N.I.S	23	7.75 N.I.S
MEDIUM	9.50 N.I.S	30	11.00 N.I.S
LARGE	12.50 N.I.S	38	14.45 N.I.S
EXTRA LARGE	15.50 N.I.S	45	17.75 N.I.S
	SUPER PIZZA		
SMALL	8.65 N.I.S	30	9.95 N.I.S
MEDIUM	9.65 N.I.S	35	10.95 N.I.S
LARGE	11.65 N.I.S	40	12.95 N.I.S
	MC PIZZA		
SMALL	6.95 N.I.S	25	1 N.I.S
LARGE	9.95 N.I.S	35	1.25 N.I.S

Figure 1. Authentic task to assess students' solutions

The Pizza Task is familiar to junior high school students, the mathematical data is rich and there is no ready-made algorithm for solution. It requires the use of a variety of sources of information (e.g., prices, size, number of supplements), and has many different correct solutions. The solvers must make computations, use different representations and apply knowledge regarding geometry, fractions and ratio.

Students' responses were scored on three criteria based on the model of Cai, Lane and Jakabcsin (1996) for analysing open-ended tasks: (a) processing information; (b) using mathematical strategies; and (c) using mathematical communication. Each criterion was scored between 0 (no response or incorrect response) to 5 (full correct response). A full, correct answer calls for organizing the information in a table, diagram, or an algebraic expression, making a correct suggestion based on the given information, and justifying the suggestion by explaining one's mathematical reasoning. Inter-judge reliability of four categories was .89.

4. RESULTS

Table 1 presents the scores, and standard deviations on problem solving of the authentic tasks by time and treatment. A one way MANCOVA was carried out on the various measures of the authentic task with the pre-test scores used as a covariant.

Table 1. Mean scores and standard deviation on the pre-test and post-test by treatment

		EMAIL + META N= 28	EMAIL N= 33	CONTROL N=36	
Pre-test Prior knowledge	M	81.81	79.70	77.80	$F(2,94)=.05$ $P>.05$
	SD	15.20	17.21	14.81	
Post-test Authentic pizza task	M	44.01	30.16	25.22	$F(2,93)=10.81$ $P<.0001$
	SD	20.78	18.8	12.28	
Adjusted M		38.95	32.05	27.82	
Processing information	M	19.64	10.94	10.42	$F(2,93)=12.38$ $P<.0001$
	SD	10.58	8.70	7.76	
Adjusted M		18.86	11.58	10.38	
Using mathematical strategies	M	16.52	10.42	5.49	$F(2,93)=19.58$ $P<.0001$
	SD	10.79	8.05	5.58	
Adjusted M		15.79	11.01	5.46	
Using mathematical communication M		22.10	14,24	13.07	$F(2,93)=12.52$ $P<.0001$
SD		9.24	9.40	5.71	
Adjusted M		21.44	14.78	13.04	

Note. Range scores [a], 0-100.

Results indicated that prior to the beginning of the study no significant differences were found between the students in the three treatments on their prior knowledge. Results of the post-test indicated that students who were exposed to the EMAIL+META condition significantly outperformed their counterparts (EMAIL and CONT classes) in solving the authentic task. As expected the EMAIL+META students benefited from the metacognitive instruction on the three criteria: Processing information, using mathematical strategies and using mathematical communication, but students in the EMAIL condition without metacognitive instruction significantly outperformed their counterparts in the CONT condition only on one criterion, using mathematical strategies. No significant differences were found between the EMAIL classes and the CONT classes on the other two criteria, processing information and using mathematical communication.

5. DISCUSSION

The present study raises several questions for future research. First, how can technology be utilised to enhance cognitive development? In the light of the constructivist approach, it seems that in order to utilise advanced technologies efficiently, students should be exposed to metacognitive instruction that enhances awareness, self-control, and self-monitoring of the cognitive processes. There may be a need to design metacognitive strategies that would be an integral part of the mathematical discourse. Such questioning may lead students to activate different levels of problem solving.

The findings are in line with other results that show that metacognitive instruction enhances mathematical problem solving as well as the ability to communicate mathematical reasoning in the classrooms (Kramarski 2000) and support other conclusions on the importance of integrating pedagogical uses with advanced technology, in particular metacognitive instruction (Deaudelin and Richer 1999; Kramarski and Zeichner 2001).

The results raise two main questions: (a) "What is the role of metacognitive instruction in enhancing different aspects of authentic task solutions?" and (b) "Why did the EMAIL students not outperform the CONT students on mathematical communication?"

The metacognitive self-addressed comprehension questions ("What is the problem all about?") probably guided students to look for all the relevant information, distinguish between the relevant and irrelevant information, and comprehend the entire task rather than parts of it. The connection questions ("How is this problem/task different/similar from what you have already solved?") might lead students to pay attention to all the information and the structure of the given task. So being trained to use the self-addressed questions may have led students to focus on the structural features of the task as well as on all the information given in the task.

The findings further showed that the metacognitive students were also better able to reorganize and process given information than their counterparts in the non-metacognitive condition, probably because the metacognitive instruction trained students to think about which strategies are appropriate for solving the task and why. By doing so, students suggested different kinds of representations, compared the strategies, and analysed each strategy.

Finally, it was found that the EMAIL+META students were better able to communicate their reasoning than their counterparts in the non-metacognitive conditions, who were also encouraged to discuss their mathematical ideas and be involved in the mathematical discourse that took place in the small group. That finding indicates that using e-mail communication and face-to-face conversation are not sufficient for enhancing mathematical problem solving. Further research based on observations and e-mail discourse analysis may provide richer insight into our understanding of how students solve authentic tasks using electronic mail communication.

REFERENCES

Butler, D. L. and Winne, P. H. (1995) Feedback and self-regulated learning: A theoretical synthesis. *Review of Educational Research* 65 3 245-281.

Cai, J., Lane, S., and Jakabcsin, M. S. (1996) The role of open-ended tasks and holistic scoring rubrics: Assessing students' mathematical reasoning and communication. In P.C. Elliott and M. J. Kenney (eds.) *Communication in Mathematics, K-12 and Beyond.* New York: Academic Press 137-145.

Deaudelin, C. and Richer, A. (1999) A learning conversation approach integrating email: Its experiment to support the student learning process at college level. Paper presented at the 8th annual EARLI Conference, Goteborg, Sweden.

Kramarski, B. (2000) The effects of different instructional methods on the ability to communicate mathematical reasoning. In Tadao Nakahara and Masataka Koyama (eds.) *Proceedings of the 24th Conference of the International Group for the Psychology of Mathematics Education,* Hiroshima University: Hiroshima, Japan 1 167-171.

Kramarski, B., Mevarech, Z. R., and Liberman, A. (2001) The effects of multilevel - versus unilevel-metacognitive training on mathematical reasoning. *Journal for Educational Research* 94 5 292-300.

Kramarski, B. and Zeichner, O. (2001) Using technology to enhance mathematical reasoning: Effects of feedback and self-regulation learning. *Educational Media International* 38 2/3 77-82.

Mevarech, Z. R. and Kramarski, B. (1997) IMPROVE: A multidimensional method for teaching mathematics in heterogeneous classrooms. *American Educational Research Journal* 34 2 365-395.

National Council of Teachers of Mathematics. (2000) *Principles and Standards for School Mathematics*. Reston, VA: National Council of Teachers of Mathematics.

OECD. (2000) *Measuring Students Knowledge and Skills*. The PISA 2000 Assessment of Reading, Mathematical and Scientific Literacy. Paris: OECD.

Schoenfeld, A. H. (1992) Learning to think mathematically: Problem solving, metacognition, and sense making in mathematics. In D. A. Grouws (ed.) *Handbook of Research on Mathematics Teaching and Learning*. New York: MacMillan 165-197.

Symons, S. and Greene, C. (1993) Elaborative interrogation and children's learning of unfamiliar facts. *Applied Cognitive Psychology* 7 219-228.

Webb, N. M. (1991). Task-related verbal interaction and mathematics learning in small groups. *Journal for Research in Mathematics Education* 22 366-389.

BIOGRAPHY

Bracha Kramarski is an expert in mathematical education in different learning environments. Her main interests are the teaching of mathematics, new technologies, cognition and metacognition, and teacher training. She also developed programs for the teaching of mathematics in different environments — the development and management of a project, IMPROVE Method for teaching mathematics in classrooms, for example. She is currently Deputy Director of the School of Education and Head of the Teachers Training and In-Service Education at Bar-Ilan University, Israel.

Adiva Liberman is a research assistant and specializes in developing materials within the IMPROVE method.

Online searching as apprenticeship

Young people and web search strategies

Matthew Pearson

School of Education and Professional Development, University of Huddersfield, Queensgate, Huddersfield, HD1 3DH, UK; m.j.pearson@hud.ac.uk

Abstract: To participate in the Information Society, it is necessary to acquire online searching skills. Despite the promise of improved searching software and the promises of instant access to information made by the search engines themselves, the process still requires human cognition. Many studies of searching behaviour have been made and are summarised along with a report of current research on group interviews with 10 year-old school children. Attitudes to searching the web and negotiating the various digital repositories of information available to them provide valuable clues about children's e-learning. A significant finding was the lack of distinction made between resources held on local machines, those on the school network and those on the Internet itself. Analysed from a phenomenographic point of view, it appears that young people are concerned about protecting their own data and privacy, and often those concerns override the need to find new information. Searching was not seen as an activity in its own right; instead, young people concentrated on identifying sources that were usable in a given context. Also of importance was the role of social collaboration, both with siblings and parents, in web searching.

Key words: elementary education, learning styles, social contexts, research

1. INTRODUCTION

An information society can only function when citizens are able to gain free access to information, and shape it for their own ends — search and use retrieval skills, display the ability to process information, make sense of it, and manipulate it into new forms. Understanding how children become enculturated into such practices is the central theme of this essay. The World

Wide Web (WWW) is currently one of the most tangible manifestations of our struggle with information: A frontier where we encounter the enormity of the information on the Internet in all its disorganised glory. Despite the hype that creates metaphors such as "information at your fingertips", or that conceptualises the web as an online library with an innate sense of order, the web is a complex and chaotic space, and our interactions with it are far from straightforward. Dreyfus (2001), drawing on the philosophy of Merleau-Ponty, discusses how our physical bodies allow us to make sense of the world and how those intuitive heuristic processes that are a function of our physical being in the world are dislocated in virtual settings. He continues his philosophical essay by examining the failure of computer scientists to produce intelligent search instruments for the web, and deconstructs the promise of agents powered by Artificial Intelligence (AI) that can search the web and bring relevant information straight back to our desktops:

> There is a vast and ever-growing field of information out there, and it looks like our only access to it will have to be through computers that don't share our bodies, don't share our world and so don't understand the meaning of our documents and web sites. (Dreyfus 2001)

Dreyfus, stoutly refusing to accept the promises of AI, reminds us that searching the web will continue to require human skills, knowledge and perhaps even guile. The search engines, despite their promise of information on demand, are nothing more than unthinking brutes, delivering thousands of pages that contain certain words but do not enable us make sense of what has been retrieved. According to Dreyfus, making sense of information and sorting it into usable forms will be a task for human cognition for many years to come. And so the ability to search the web for relevant information may become one of the central skills for participants in the information society.

Moreover, given the rhetorical promises attached to young people, in which they are constructed as the next generation of cyber citizens and the natural heirs of a digital future, it is important that we find out how children learn to search the web and navigate their way around complex information spaces. This entails more than just noting which search engines they use, how they organise their search behaviour and how they develop criteria for successful searches. We need to look beyond the procedural aspects of searching, and understand the ways in which young people represent the information spaces through which they navigate and how they harness cognitive processes to conduct searches.

2. CHILDREN'S SEARCHING STRATEGIES

Given the importance of finding what we need to find on the web, not surprisingly there is already a considerable amount of research on searching behaviour, including some studies done with children. Studies fall broadly into three categories: The first category consists of studies that seek to explain search behaviour and analyse search strategies in terms of their constituent components (for example, White and Iivonen 2001); the second category includes studies where the searching of experts is compared with less-experienced searchers "newbies" (Hölscher and Strube 2000); the third category includes studies involving the development of new software or tools to assist in searching (Spink 2002).

A useful summary of studies on web searching can be found in Hsieh-Lee (2001), reporting on most of the work done to date and highlighting the work of Bilal (1998), who found notable weaknesses summarised by Hsieh-Lee:

> ... although they understand the given task, children did not search efficiently or effectively and their search paths revealed frequent looping, back-tracking and poor navigation (Hsieh-Lee 2001).

Children seem to search the web in an ad hoc and random way, and there is a faint tone of reproach, an undercurrent of criticism for feckless youth who will not adopt appropriate search strategies. But perhaps children are serving an apprenticeship as information retrieval experts during this stage, and, true to the form of apprentices, they sometimes cut corners, fail to realise what is important and don't always work with the fastidious exactness of the masters.

My work with children searching the web suggests that they do have many sophisticated searching skills, but expecting them to reach adult competence, and measuring them against this standard is not helpful in understanding how they learn to search (Pearson, 2002). In fact this paper will argue that children who have been brought up with the Internet and the web do not immediately perceive a difference between searching on the web and searching other digital repositories. So research into searching behaviour in different ways might take a more holistic view of information retrieval, and not one which concentrates on the web alone.

Studies of searching behaviour that are modelled too closely on adults' interactions with the web may fail to account for fundamental differences in the ways in which children conceptualise the web. The research on searching behaviour and the efforts at improving the quality of search strategies is likely to grow dramatically as policy makers, software designers, educationalists, and any one else with a stake in the information society, realise that unless people are able to find and use information, all the promise of a virtual economy comes to naught.

Facer, et al. (2001) have examined in detail the discursive structures that surround children's computer use, as well as some of the contradictions which constrict children as both experts, fully at home in the digital world and able to exercise agency and self-control, and, simultaneously, as passive consumers of digital culture.

The act of searching the web is a curious mixture of procedural activity (find a search engine, enter key terms, review results, click links to visit sites), high level cognitive endeavour (the information density on an average page of search results is extremely high and requires a great deal of processing), and pure stochastic incidence (sometimes you just hit on the correct site by chance). The technology of the search engine presents itself as being easy to use, and the popular search engine Ask Jeeves employs the conceit of a butler who can be sent off on data collection "errands" and who dutifully delivers the goods right to our desktops. Any hint of the weaknesses in web searching and of promises which cannot be kept are eschewed from the interface altogether. Advanced search engine features such as Boolean operators and domain specific searches are nearly always not given on the front page of the site, and require the click of the "advanced" button. The search itself takes only seconds and somehow the list of hits, although constructed at lightning speed, has an authority which makes us respond as if to a definitive list of sites.

Expert searchers, because they can draw upon knowledge of how search engines operate, can move beyond that allure of authority and will perform repeated searches, refining terms and adjusting criteria to improve relevance. Hale and Moss (1999) coined the term "hazyspace" to capture the sense of a list of information which may or may not be relevant to the task in hand and which needs considerable expertise on the part of searchers to reach their teleological goals.

So, despite the popular view of the web as an encyclopaedia, digital library or information store, where searching is a transparent and irrelevant precursor to getting our hands on the information, searching is what the web is all about. Only users who can navigate through the complex of information will be able to take a full part in the Information Society. Searching may seem like consumption of information, the web equivalent of flicking channels on a satellite TV receiver until something interesting is found, but it is an active wrestling with information requiring an active cognitive engagement with the material and a huge wealth of supporting skills and knowledge. Despite discourses that construct our searching as trouble-free interactions modelled on transparent consumption, web searching is a difficult business.

2.1 Research on children's interactions with information sources

Early stages of research conducted with 9 and 10 year-old school children in the United Kingdom (Pearson 2002) is predicated on constructivist principles, and the design of the methodology has been driven by the belief that children actively construct mental representations of the technology they encounter. The research also shows that children's representations further developed their expertise. Folk psychology has already enshrined such principles in the popular imagination by saying children do not need to "read the manual", they "just pick it up as they go along", and "they are the only ones who can program the video."

The early plan for the present research study was to use a phenomenographic approach to data collection and analysis. Pioneered by Marton (1994), the research method seeks to categorise ways in which phenomena are experienced and, from the categorisations, draw conclusions about learning. Phenomenography seeks to differentiate between deep and surface learning, and by focussing on the perceptual efforts of the learners, attempts to draw distinctions between the core, fields and fringes of experience.

The first data collection encounters with the young people took the form of very informal group interviews in the computer suite of their school. Pressure on schools to achieve and maintain high Standard Assessment Test (SAT) scores has made it difficult to gain access to children, especially where access may entail taking them away from core curriculum subjects. So I visited the school during lunchtimes, when a group of 9 and 10 year-old pupils were allowed to use the computers and participate in the research. The early encounters had a deliberate lack of structure as I sought to understand a little more about how the children were using the computers and what issues were important for them. In conversation with them it became clear that searching the web was not an important issue and some even expressed surprise that I wanted to know about it. What also emerged was the children's lack of differentiation between resources that were available online and those stored on local hard drives or the school network. In response to a direct question about how they found things on the web, the following answer was given:

> When you need to find something out, then click on this (agitates mouse pointer over the icon which launches MS

> Encarta), or just go here (indicates the web browser icon), go to Ask Jeeves, and then you'll just get straight to the stuff .... (male age 10, Pearson 2002)

For him, the information available from the desktop of the school computer did not fall into the categories of local, network and Internet resource. The phrase "go straight to the stuff" combines both immediacy and informality, and demonstrates that at this point the boy did not see searching as a discrete activity. Indeed, when pressed to explain a little more about the various sources the same student replied:

> Encarta is like the best bit of the Internet on these machines, these bits (motions towards a web page which has been loading for the last 5 minutes and has now stalled) take forever to load, but Encarta comes up really quickly. (Pearson 2002)

His point of view is not factually correct. The Encarta CD runs on the school network (hence the retrieval speed), and although there are links outward to the Internet, it is essentially a local resource. In phenomenographic terms, the children did not experience the various sources of information available to them as differentiated phenomena. Whether an information source was online or local or networked was a fringe concern, and the core of their cognitive activity was directed towards finding information that was accessible. In the school where the research was taking place, Internet access had been poor for many months, and many of the young people interviewed had ceased to bother opening browsers, concentrating instead on locally networked resources.

The failure to discriminate between different aspects of the digital network coincides with the findings of Somekh and Pearson (2001), who used concept maps to explore 10 year-old children's mental representations of digital technology. The study found that children drew maps with very high levels of interconnectivity and elements belonging to the Internet were connected with other devices and other networks. Somekh and Pearson (2001) also found many concept maps in which mobile phones, games consoles and even cars and watches were all linked to a central node represented by an iconic globe character which represented the Internet. Distinctions between various elements of networks and factual elements representing the true nature of connectivity were rare and most children's maps focussed instead on how various elements of technology are becoming joined up by networking.

As the group interviews and informal data collection sessions progressed (there were a total of five over a period of two weeks), gradually the concerns of the young people regarding their use of ICT emerged. An entirely different agenda from that of searching for information surfaced, one that foregrounded the young people's own data and work, and was tied in with their concerns about safety and privacy. All children had access to their own server space on the school network, referring to that space as the gateway, and they jealously guarded their passwords and user privileges. This anxiety about keeping data secret, or of circumventing possible unauthorised access by other pupils or surveillance by teachers, often extended into the home:

> On my dad's machine I have my own folders. I learned how to put a password on them and now only I can see inside. My dad didn't know how I'd done this, but I won't let him have the password, I don't want him looking at my stuff. (female, age 10, Pearson 2002)

The theme of data security surfaced again and again. It shows that the children's engagements with ICT were often driven by the need to make a personal space and retain possession of their own data, rather than searching the web for information. Searching the web was seen as an important activity by most but few of the participants in the study could explain how search engines worked or reflect in any detail on their searching behaviour. Another significant theme that emerged during the group interviewing process was the role of collaboration, especially in the home, in finding materials on the web. The following quotations, from two children, point to the roles of parents and siblings in helping children of this age locate web pages:

> If I want something, my Dad just goes click click click (mimes someone typing very fast on the keyboard), and there it is. He then saves it onto my special page which has all my favourite sites on. (female, age 10, Pearson 2002)

> Me and my brother look for things together, PlayStation games or CDs or sometimes football results. He controls the mouse, and we decide where to click next. (male, age 9, Pearson 2002)

3. CONCLUSION

Distinctions between the Internet, the World Wide Web, local and network resources were not routinely made by the young people in this study. Rather than categorising resources by type, they saw only the accessibility of information from the school's computers as being the issue. Thus CD-ROMs and local resources were favoured over Internet resources primarily because of the speed of loading of the former, and the glacially slow download of the latter. The children interviewed all expressed considerable frustration at the failings of the school's Internet connection, and eight out of the ten, who had regular access to the Internet at home, made direct and unfavourable comparisons between ease of access in the home and the failure of the school network. More research is needed in this area, and it will be necessary to understand more about how children mentally represent the various digital resources available to them and how they make decisions about utilising them. Finally, to understand more about how young people search for resources, it will be necessary to capture the social component of searching. That aspect, all too often lost in experimental studies which force users into individual modes of action, is clearly important, and may tell us much more about how young people become enculturated into information societies.

REFERENCES

Bilal, D. (1998) Children's search processes in using World Wide Web search engines: An exploratory study. In C. M. Preston (ed.) *Proceedings of the 61st ASIS Annual Meeting*. Medford, NJ: Information Today 45-51.

Dreyfus, H. L. (2001) *On the Internet*. Routledge: London.

Facer, K., Furlong, J., Furlong, R., and Sutherland, R. (2001) Constructing the child computer user: From public policy to private practices. *British Journal of Sociology of Education* 22 1 91-108.

Hale, G. and Moss, N. (1999) Methodological issues in using grounded theory to investigate Internet searching. Paper presented at the European Conference Educational Research 25th conference, September 1999.

Hölscher, C., and Strube, G. (2000) Web search behaviour of Internet experts and newbies. *Computer Networks* 33 337-346.

Hsieh-Yee, I. (2001) Research on Web search behavior. *Library and Information Science Research* 23 167-185.

Marton, F. (1994) Phenomenography. In T. Husen and T. N. Postlethwaite (eds.) *The International Encyclopedia of Education*. Oxford: Pergamon 8 4424-4427.

Pearson, M. (2002) Children's search strategies. Unpublished paper.

Somekh, B. and Pearson, M. (2001) Children's representations of new technology: Mismatches between the Public Education Curriculum and socio-cultural learning. Paper presented at the *American Educational Research Association Annual Conference*: Seattle, WA, April 2001.

Spink, A (2002) A user-centered approach to evaluating human interaction with Web search engines: An exploratory study. *Information Processing and Management* 38 3 401-426.

White, M. D. and Iivonen, M. (2001) Questions as a factor in Web search strategy. *Information Processing and Management* 37 5 721-740.

BIOGRAPHY

Matthew Pearson studied English Literature before completing a Ph.D. in modern literary theory. He then trained as an English teacher and taught in sixth form colleges. During that time he developed an interest in ICT and began to experiment in using technology for teaching purposes. He is now a senior lecturer at the University of Huddersfield, where he is course leader for a Masters degree in Multimedia and Education. His research interests are now centred on the ways young people use digital technologies.

The use of virtual reality three-dimensional simulation technology in nursery school teacher training for the understanding of children's cognitive perceptions

Yaacov J. Katz
School of Education, Bar-Ilan University, Ramat-Gan 52900, Israel; katzya@mail.biu.ac.il

Abstract: This study examined the effectiveness and efficiency of a three-dimensional virtual reality simulation model designed to train nursery school teachers in the understanding of nursery school children's cognitive perceptions. An experimental group of 45 nursery school teachers underwent 20 hours of virtual reality simulation as opposed to 20 hours of workshop activity experienced by 44 nursery school teachers in a comparable control group. Both methodologies were designed to promote improved understanding of children's cognitive perceptions. After the training sessions the teachers were observed in their nursery school work over a period of two days by three nursery school supervisors who evaluated the research subjects' understanding of nursery school teacher's cognitive perceptions.

Statistical analysis of the data indicate that the nursery school teachers who were trained through the virtual reality simulation technology were significantly more understanding of children's cognitive perceptions and needs than those trained through the workshop method. Thus, in light of the results of the study, it is suggested that teacher trainers should favourably consider using virtual reality simulation models in the training of nursery school teachers in order to maximise the effectiveness of the teacher training process.

Key words: learning styles, teacher education

1. INTRODUCTION

Information and Communication Technology (ICT) has the potential to significantly contribute to the improvement of learning and teaching at all levels in the educational system. The development of highly sophisticated computer-based tools provides the educational system with rich potential for the development of more effective and efficient learning and teaching which, if successfully utilised, could lead to the hoped for educational revolution.

2. VIRTUAL REALITY

Among the state-of-the-art technological packages that have been made available to educators and learners are virtual reality (VR) technologies. Turman and Matton (1994) defined virtual reality as a highly interactive computer-based multimedia environment in which the user becomes a full-fledged partner in a virtual world. When experiencing virtual reality the user becomes an immersed participant in the computer-generated VR program. Bricken and Byrne (1992) stated that in order to enter into the world of virtual reality the learner wears a computerised helmet and gloves, which allow him/her to see, hear, and touch other objects in the virtual world. When the learner enters the virtual world s/he usually perceives the virtual world as a place in which s/he is physically immersed (Henry 1992). Regain and Shebliske (1992) reported that learners who enter a virtual world undergo physical and emotional experiences very similar to those that exist in the physical world.

2.1 Simulation

One of the major methodologies used in virtual reality is that of simulation and modelling (Van Weert 1995). Educational computer simulations are based on dynamic interactions between the learner and a computer program, and may be defined as that part of the modelling process which involves the execution of a model by the learner. The learner experiments with the simulated phenomenon by observing and analysing interactions between him/herself and the modelled phenomenon (Baranauskas and De Oliveira 1995). A number of studies have indicated that simulation is a rich and sophisticated computer-based learning environment that allows the learner to experience the learning situation in an encompassing, motivating and novel world. Simulation systems mimic the phenomenon under study and the learner's typical role is to discover, through a process of investigation, the rules that govern the phenomenon. The learner enters a powerful learning environment and engages in a cycle of expression, evaluation, and reflection (Schecker 1993). White (1993) described how learners who undertook animated simulation tasks in the physics of velocity were able to overcome common misconceptions that existed after studying in a traditional non-simulation environment, and Leary (1995) reported that a number of studies have indicated that learners' educational achievements through the teaching medium of simulation are higher than achievements attained after undergoing other non-simulation methods of instruction.

Cumming, Zangari and Thomason (1995) postulated that there are a number of basic assumptions that underlie the presumption that the learner will be able to derive more benefit from computer-based simulation than from other learning environments. These assumptions conclude that:

- the learner is capable of taking initiative and exploring — the simulated phenomenon provides a rich platform for the activities;
- learner engagement is all important — in simulation learner engagement is maximised by a sophisticated three-dimensional interface design that provides the learner with motivating as well as challenging activities;
- learning may be regarded as conceptual change — simulation facilitates conceptual change more efficiently than many other learning environments; learning is superior when the learner can experience both abstract and concrete aspects of the content under study — in simulations both abstract and concrete learning take place.

3. TEACHERS' UNDERSTANDING OF CHILDREN'S COGNITIVE PERCEPTIONS

Deen (1995) indicated that teaching in general is a process of understanding the pupils' cognitive perceptions. Teachers who are able to acquire this understanding are those who best cognitively empathise with their pupils, and are best equipped to assist them in the development of learning and problem-solving behaviour. According to data based on a longitudinal investigation conducted by Kikas (1998), teachers who understand their pupils' cognitive perceptions are more capable of assisting the pupils in problem-solving behaviour than teachers who have a lower level of understanding. Kikas confirmed that effective teaching is based on the confidence of teachers that they are able to understand the cognitive perceptions of their pupils and are consequently able to efficiently promote positive cognitive and problem-solving behaviours among their pupils. Calvert and Henderson (1994) stated that in order to equip teachers more comprehensively for their teaching tasks, they should undergo training in understanding the cognitive perceptions of their pupils. Bell (1998) concurred and added that effective teachers offer their pupils a varied range of rich cognitive experiences based on their deep understanding of their pupils' cognitive perceptions. Thus, in light of the evidence, it is logical to propose that teacher-training methods that are able to significantly contribute to teachers' familiarity with pupils' cognitive perceptions are the most effective and efficient.

3.1 Teachers' understanding of nursery school children's cognitive perceptions

Katznelson (1993) emphasised the potential traumas associated with the transition of the child from home or baby care centre to the more formal educational framework of the nursery school. The change that is experienced by the young child during the course of the transition can cause anxiety, fear, regression and even disorientation. Katznelson also indicated that the quality of assistance the child receives from the nursery school teacher in order to alleviate the problems associated with the transition to the new formal educational framework is dependent on the nursery school teacher's ability to fully understand the child's cognitive perceptions and to empathise with him/her.

Davies (1991) also addressed the problems that children entering nursery school may experience when entering their new educational framework, and pointed out that the nursery school is the first educational framework that makes basic cognitive demands of children and initially they may have difficulty coping with those demands. He also said that the better equipped a nursery school teacher is to deal with the cognitive perceptions of children beginning their nursery school year, the more competent the teacher is in contributing to the alleviation of children's problems. Rubinstein (1990) postulated that an important aspect of nursery school teachers' educational roles is to familiarise children with the cognitive demands of the new nursery school environment in order to allay anxieties and fear induced by the transition into a new and potentially threatening complex learning situation.

In his theory of cognitive development Piaget (1978) described in detail the different developmental stages that a child goes through from birth until late adolescence, during which the child's cognitive ability steadily develops. Basing their work on Piaget's developmental model, Glover and Bruning (1987) described the cognitive development and perceptions of the nursery school child. They indicated that nursery school children do not perceive their environment objectively and their perceptions are different from those of adults. Nursery school children categorise objects while using unitary characteristics, and are unable to view the cognitive world from a viewpoint other than their own because their reasoning tends to be egocentric. Adult cognition is based on formal operations, abstract thought and multifaceted categorisation of situations. Thus adult reasoning does not remotely resemble the cognitive patterns of a child and will not be effective when trying to understand the nursery school child's cognitive perceptions because of the vast developmental gap that exists between the two age groups. Phillips (1975) remarked that adults wishing to understand young children's cognitive perceptions must set aside their cognitive models and attempt to enter children's cognitive world. Without competent adult understanding of the nursery school child's cognitive processes, the cognitive gap between young children and adults will strongly mitigate against mutual understanding and perceptions.

4. AIM OF THE RESEARCH PROJECT

From the review of the literature it is apparent that teachers who better understand pupils' cognitive perceptions are more capable of assisting their pupils in a variety of difficult and problematic situations that arise in the cognitive domain. It is also apparent that the computer-based technology of virtual reality, which uses three-dimensional simulation as an instructional methodology, has many advantages over other more traditional and non-technological instructional methodologies regarding the level of understanding attained by the learner. Thus the aim of the present study was to investigate whether instruction through the medium of a virtual reality three-dimensional simulation model effectively provides nursery school teachers with the ability to better understand children's cognitive development, perceptions and needs.

5. METHOD

5.1 Sample

The research sample consisted of 89 female nursery school teachers in their first year of teaching after obtaining a B.Ed. degree in nursery school teaching at accredited teacher training colleges. At the time of the research, during the 2001 academic year, all 89 subjects were engaged in a year-long in-service training course provided by the Division of Educational Technology in partnership with the Division of In-Service Teacher Training at the School of Education, Bar-Ilan University. During the period of their in-service training the 89 teachers agreed to participate in the present research study and 45 were randomly allocated to the experimental group and 44 to the control group.

5.2 Instruments

A research questionnaire designed to examine the subjects' understanding of children's cognitive perceptions and needs was specially compiled. The first draft of the questionnaire consisted of 36 items arranged on a five-point Likert Scale and was presented to three expert university professors who specialise in nursery school teacher training for face and content validity evaluation. The items that met the validity criteria used by the expert evaluators were included in the final version of the research questionnaire.

5.3 Hardware

The hardware used for the virtual reality simulation included a PC Pentium III computer, a head-mounted display HMD helmet fitted with two video screens placed in the helmet eyepieces for stereoscopic vision, a stereophonic 360° 3-D Audio Reality kit for each ear, a virtual reality glove for changing the position of objects in the virtual world, and a tracking system for placement of the user in the virtual environment.

5.4 Software

The software consisted of a Super Scape® (Version 5.5) package that managed all the virtual reality activities and interfaces. The software facilitates the building of immersive three-dimensional virtual environments that are viewed with the HMD helmet, heard when using the Audio Reality kit, and manipulated by way of the virtual reality glove.

6. PROCEDURE

The design of the research was quasi-experimental with a post-test only evaluation of the 89 research subjects' performance in the nursery school classroom undertaken after their period of in-service training. During their period of in-service training, each of the 45 subjects in the experimental group and the 44 subjects in the control group underwent instruction designed to increase their understanding of nursery school children's cognitive perceptions and needs according to the developmental model proposed by Piaget (1978). The content matter studied in the in-service training program emphasised the cognitive perceptions relevant to nursery school children's cognitive development, the thought processes characterising the level of cognitive development at the pre-operational stage, and the idiosyncratic phenomena associated with that development.

The experimental group subjects experienced 20 hours of training through the medium of a computer-based virtual reality module that simulated three-dimensionally how nursery school children cognitively perceive their surroundings and their learning tasks within the nursery school environment.

Each teacher in the experimental group was transported into a three-dimensional virtual environment that simulated the nursery school child's cognitive world and demonstrated how a child perceives and understands that world. Thus the experimental group subjects experienced for themselves, in a virtual environment, the cognitive problems facing nursery school children in the real world, and experienced pre-operational cognitive perceptions and needs. For example, they perceived the furniture present in the nursery school classroom from the perspective of a nursery school child and not from the perspective of an adult. The teachers' perceptions of the educational equipment such as pencils, crayons, drawing paper, and educational toys they used in the simulated virtual environment closely resembled the perceptions of nursery school children using the same equipment in their nursery school classrooms. Learning tasks, such as elementary writing and reading skills taught in the nursery school, and the construction of models using building blocks, were experienced by the teachers exactly as nursery school children experienced the same learning tasks. In this way the 45 research subjects perceived and experienced cognitive stimuli presented in the virtual world just as if they themselves were of nursery school age.

The control group participated in 20 hours of orientation workshops run by nursery school teaching instructors who conveyed to them (without the use of technology) how nursery school children perceive their cognitive world. Children's problems and cognitive difficulties were brought to the subjects' attention and they received detailed explanations regarding the children's pre-operational cognitive perceptions and needs. The subjects were instructed about nursery school children's cognitive and spatial problems and the difficulties they face when attempting the typical cognitive learning tasks undertaken at the nursery school level.

Thereafter, three Israeli Ministry of Education nursery school supervisors, who acted as evaluators of the nursery school teachers participating in the study, completed questionnaires for each of the 89 nursery school teachers in both experimental and control groups without knowing each subject's group placement.

The three supervisors were chosen as evaluators of the teachers since they were responsible for both supervision and guidance of the 89 research subjects in their respective nursery school classrooms throughout the school year and, in the course of their supervisory roles, met weekly with each of the 89 teachers in order to assist them with the planning and implementation of their routine teaching duties.

The task of the supervisors in the study was to evaluate the efficiency and effectiveness of the nursery school teachers' instructional abilities and their overall suitability to serve as nursery school teachers with special emphasis on their specific understanding of nursery school children's cognitive perceptions and needs.

The supervisors completed the questionnaires after observing each of the nursery school teachers in their nursery school classrooms over a period of three full teaching days after the teachers had completed the training designed to acquaint them with nursery school children's cognitive perceptions as required. In their evaluations the three supervisors specifically concentrated on the evaluation of all relevant aspects of the nursery school teachers' understanding of children's cognitive perceptions and needs in the nursery school learning situation.

After evaluating the 89 nursery school teachers in the research sample by completing a questionnaire for each research subject, the supervisors' evaluations were factor analysed in a principal components analysis and the 16 items that met the criterion of statistical significance (.30) were used in the statistical analysis of the research data. The 16 items clustered around one significant factor, which was labelled "nursery school teachers' understanding of children's cognitive perceptions". The factor had a latent root greater than unity and explained at least 10 percent of the variance. The Cronbach alpha reliability coefficient of the "nursery school teachers' understanding of children's cognitive perceptions" variable reached the 0.91 level.

7. RESULTS

Group means for experimental and control groups for the "nursery school teachers' understanding of children's cognitive perceptions" variable were computed from data collected from the nursery school supervisors' evaluations of the research subjects during three days of observation of how the subjects dealt with children's cognitive perceptions and needs in the course of their work. The group means were then compared in a t-test analysis calculated for independent samples. The results of the t-test are presented in Table 1.

Table 1. T-test for independent samples for "Nursery School Teachers' Level of Understanding of Children's Cognitive Perceptions" variable

Group	N	Mean	S.D.	D.F.	t	P
VR instruction	45	41.11	2.49	87	11.23	P<0.001
Workshop instruction	44	36.47	2.43			

Results of the t-test indicate that the nursery school teachers in the experimental group who received instruction about nursery school children's cognitive perceptions and needs through a virtual reality 3-D simulation received significantly higher evaluations of their understanding of the children's cognitive perceptions and needs than nursery school teachers belonging to the control group.

8. DISCUSSION

Results of the statistical analysis conducted on the data collected from the evaluations of the three nursery school supervisors of the subjects in the experimental and control groups participating in the study show that the nursery school teachers who underwent 20 hours of 3-D simulation in a virtual reality environment received superior evaluations of their understanding of children's cognitive perceptions and needs than the teachers who went through 20 hours of workshop experience on the cognitive perceptions of nursery school children. According to the supervisors' evaluations, the experimental group teachers were more sensitive to the children's cognitive needs and exhibited significantly higher levels of understanding towards them than the teachers in the control group.

The results of the study suggest that sophisticated technology used in the experiment has the advantage of immersing the adult nursery school teacher in the nursery school children's world, thereby better acquainting the teachers with that world. The result is congruent with White's (1993) research describing how learners who undertook animated simulation tasks in the physics of velocity were able to overcome common misconceptions that existed after studying the principles of velocity in a traditional non-simulation environment, and, as a result, better understood the content matter and also seems to confirm the results of studies reported by Leary (1995) indicating that learners' achievements through the teaching medium of simulation are higher than achievements attained after undergoing other non-simulation methods of instruction.

The results of the study indicate that learning and instruction through the medium of a sophisticated technology platform comprising a 3-D simulation in a virtual world have the potential to prepare nursery school teachers more effectively and efficiently for their roles. Their understanding of children's cognitive perceptions is significantly superior to the skills developed when nursery school teachers learn through the medium of more traditional, non-technological methods such as workshops.

REFERENCES

Baranauskas, M.C. and De Oliveira, O.L. (1995) Domain oriented modeling: A balance between simulation and programming. In J.D. Tinsley and T.J. van Weert (eds.) *Liberating the Learner: Proceedings of the Sixth IFIP World Conference on Computers in Education, 1995.* London: Chapman and Hall 119-126.

Bell, G. (1998) The personal effectiveness program initiative. *Pastoral Care in Education* 16 2 20-26.

Bricken, M. and Byrne, C.M. (1992) Summer Students in Virtual Reality: A Pilot Study on Educational Applications of Virtual Reality Technology. Seattle, WA: University of Washington http://www.hitl.washington.edu/projects/education/.

Calvert, M. and Henderson, J. (1994) Newly qualified teachers: Do we prepare them for their pastoral role? *Pastoral Care in Education* 12 2 7-12.

Cumming, G., Zangari, M. and Thomason, N. (1995) Designing software for cognitive change: Statplay and understanding statistics. In J.D. Tinsley and T.J. van Weert (eds.) *Liberating the Learner: Proceedings of the Sixth IFIP World Conference on Computers in Education, 1995.* London: Chapman and Hall 753-765.

Davies, J. (1991) Children's adjustment to nursery class: How to equalise opportunities for successful experience. *School Organisation* 11 255-262.

Deen, N. (1995) Schools make people grow: Notes on the supportive school. *Pastoral Care in Education* 13 3 19-25.

Glover, J.A. and Bruning, R.H. (1987) *Educational Psychology: Principles and Applications.* Boston: Little, Brown and Company.

Henry, D. (1992) Spatial Perception in Virtual Environments: Evaluating an ArchitecturalAapplication. Seattle, WA: University of Washington. http://www.hitl.washington.edu/projects/education/.

Katznelson, A. (1993) When it happens. *Parents and Children* 67 17-18 (Hebrew).

Kikas, E. (1998) The impact of teaching on students' definitions and explanations of astronomical phenomena. *Learning and Instruction* 8 5 439-454.

Leary, J.J. (1995) Computer simulated laboratory experiments and computer games: A designer's analysis. In J.D. Tinsley and T.J. van Weert (Eds.) *Liberating the Learner: Proceedings of the Sixth IFIP World Conference on Computers in Education, 1995.* London: Chapman and Hall 963-973.

Phillips, J.L. (1975) *The Origins of Intellect: Piaget's Theory* (2nd ed.). San Francisco, CA: Freeman.

Piaget, J. (1978) A summary of the theory of Jean Piaget. In D.K. Gardiner (ed.) *Readings in Developmental Psychology.* New York: Holt 3-23.

Regain, J.W. and Shebliske, W.L. (1992) Virtual reality: An instructional medium for visual and spatial terms. *Journal of Communication* 42 4 136-149.
Rubinstein, M. (1990) *Years of growth*. Tel-Aviv: Hadar Publishers (Hebrew).
Schecker, H. (1993) Learning physics by making models. *Physics Education* 28 102-106.
Turman, R.A. and Matton, J.S. (1994) Virtual reality: Towards improvement in simulation based training. *Educational Technology* 34 8 56-64.
Van Weert, T.J. (1995) IFIP Working Group 3.1: Towards integration of computers into education. In J.D. Tinsley and T.J. van Weert (eds.) *Liberating the Learner: Proceedings of the Sixth IFIP World Conference on Computers in Education, 1995*. London: Chapman and Hall 3-12.
White, B.Y. (1993) Thinker tools: Causal models conceptual change and science education. *Cognition and Instruction* 10 1-100.

BIOGRAPHY

Yaacov Katz is the Director of the Institute for Community Education and Research at Bar-Ilan University and serves as the Chair of the Pedagogic secretariat of the Israeli Ministry of Education. He specializes in research on attitudes of students and teachers towards different issues in the Israeli educational system, with special emphasis on attitudes toward the use of ICT in the learning and instructional processes. He has edited a number of books and written numerous scholarly papers on the above topics. He is a member of IFIP's Working Group 3.5.

Exploring visible mathematics with IMAGINE

Building new mathematical cultures with a powerful computational system

Ivan Kalas and Andrej Blaho
Department of Informatics Education, Comenius University, 842 48 Bratislava, Slovakia;kalas@fmph.unia.sk;blaho@fmph.uniba.sk

Abstract: In our paper we explore how programmable pictures together with events, parallel independent processes and direct manipulation tools can be used for building powerful interactive visual elements and provide rich environments for exploring basic mathematical concepts. To visualize the concepts we use IMAGINE turtles, the shapes of which are specified by the Logo language. Thus we achieve high interactivity in the resulting microworlds. Children can easily create such objects, control them, combine, move, group, match, etc. We hope that new features of IMAGINE will inspire math teachers and developers to create new visible math educational materials.

Key words: elementary education, organising for learning, curriculum

1. INTRODUCTION

In his inaugural lecture, Noss (1997) compared the computer to a mathematical piano, saying the computer "...can make tangible a mathematical object in much the same way that a piano can make tangible (or at least audible) the meaning of F#." He also said that powerful computational systems "... offer alternative means to express mathematical relationships, novel kinds of symbolism, and innovative ways to manipulate mathematical objects: In short, the emergence of new mathematical cultures." IMAGINE (Kalas and Blaho 2000) is such computational system with ambitions to stimulate the emergence of new cultures for constructing, exploring and understanding.

IMAGINE represents new generation of Logo. Researchers of the integration of ICT into learning processes remember that Logo always defined its goal as developing problem-solving and logical-thinking skills, and allowing young learners to build their own "intellectual structures through estimation, interaction, experience and revision" (Watt 1983). Logo has offered simple tools and mechanisms: (a) one or multiple turtles, i.e., graphical objects which have certain shapes and can draw; (b) a vocabulary of simple commands such as forward, right, etc.; and (c) a mechanism for defining the user's own procedures. The essentials allow and encourage learners to explore, create and understand.

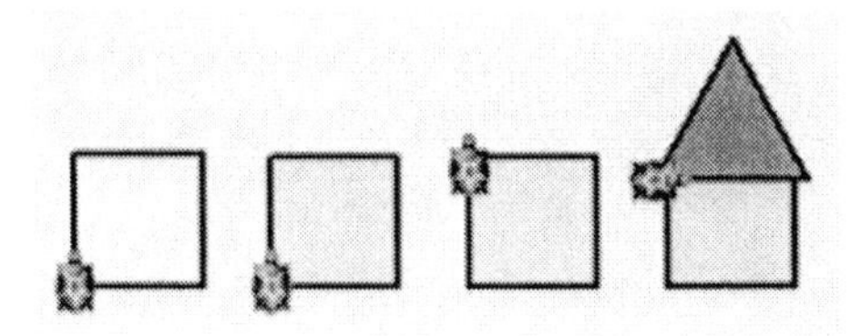

Figure 1. Traditional Logo activities

Recent developments in educational computer environments have added several new tools and techniques, as illustrated by IMAGINE. Besides traditional elements of turtle geometry as shown in Figure 1, it offers new attractive concepts for education. The new enhancements support understanding in modern exploratory mathematics, which increasingly employs creative computer environments to:

- encourage motivation in specific topics;
- explore, visualize and demonstrate relations and dependencies;
- to simulate and model;
- to act as a microworld for discovering in certain topics and as a laboratory for creating and building — e.g., a computer environment which offers a kind of smart paper with proper tools to support certain activites as shown in Figure 2, or popular environments for dynamic geometry, which offer new ways for solving traditional problems, but also completely new types of problems in the same area of explorations and new strategies how to solve them;
- as an environment for solving problems with constraints;
- for testing, etc.

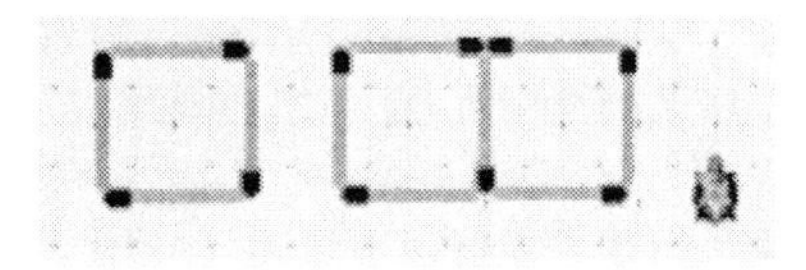

Figure 2. Smart paper with matches for exploring counts of things developed at IoE

The essential properties of IMAGINE help make mathematical objects and relations between them tangible: programmable pictures, direct manipulation tools, events, object oriented structure, and parallel independent processes, as shown in Figure 2.

1.1 Programmable pictures

Among the most interesting and innovative properties of IMAGINE is the possibility to specify shapes of turtles directly by simple Logo commands. In Kalas and Blaho (2000) we presented a broad palette of possibilities offered by this property for educational environments. All shapes specified in this way are independent of the absolute frame and thus in harmony with the traditional Logo philosophy. All programmable pictures stick to the relative frame and IMAGINE rotates them according to actual headings of turtles. Being turtles, such visual objects may easily move along the screen, change their headings, colours, sizes, speeds, etc.

We can use, for example, a well known and simple drawing of a thick red square as a description of the turtle's shape:

```
? setShape [setPenWidth 7
            setPenColour "red
            repeat 4 [fd 40 rt 90]]
```

After doing this, we have no problem with rotations of the square. It will be created automatically and online by IMAGINE itself. We can specify complex shapes which may evolve dynamically and express various mathematical objects.

What will we gain from the possibilities? Since we have used simple Logo commands to specify the shape of a turtle, we get three rewards in return: (a) the shape can be specified in exactly the same language, which we have used so far for drawing pictures; (b) we will get the shape we want — the shape can be modified any time (even while running the project); (c) this object is a Logo turtle with all related rewards such as: Easily move along the screen (or page) either by simple Logo commands like fd, bk, setPos etc., or by being dragged. It can be easily rotated by simple Logo commands right, left and setHeading, and its shape can contain lines of any colours and widths, which we set by setPenColour, setPenWidth etc., as far as we specify the shape as if drawing it by traditional turtle pen.

1.2 Direct Manipulations

Every modern programming environment for education strives to provide its users with powerful tools for direct manipulations so that young learners, students and teachers can do a lot without describing their steps through instructions of the language itself. Although IMAGINE successfully lifted the ceiling of direct manipulations from SuperLogo, its previous Logo version (Blaho, Kalas and Matusova 1994; Blaho and Kalas 1998), both IMAGINE and SuperLogo keep the same rule: Whatever can be done through direct manipulations, can exactly be expressed in Logo instructions.

Direct manipulations help us in exploring visible mathematics in two distinct ways. Either they are built in more complex application to help the learner to interact with it by clicking, dragging, giving voice commands, communicating through dialog boxes, etc. or they support the developer himself/herself so that he/she can efficiently create and modify the IMAGINE application. Properties, which help in both ways, are, for example, creating clones of objects. We can right click the object – either a simple or very complex one – and copy it into Clipboard. If we then right click into any page or any pane and choose Paste from Clipboard command, we create a clone as shown in Figure 3.

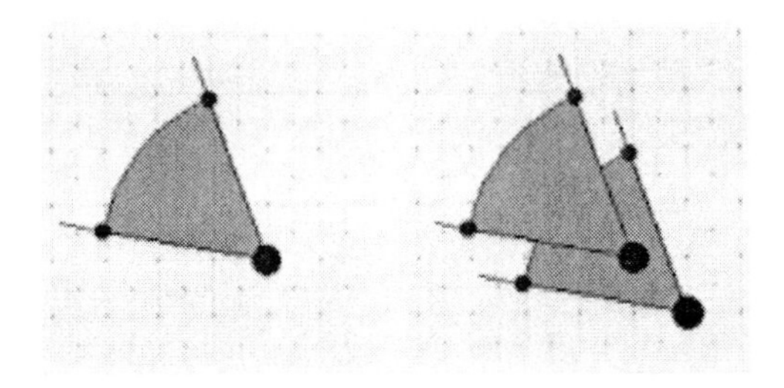

Figure 3. Clones of objects created by cut and paste through Clipboard

The page itself is an object with its own settings like background colour and background picture. If we right click the page and choose the Load background... command, the background picture can be specified, for example by a bitmap to be tiled all over the page. In this way, a useful grid of points can easily be created in the page as shown in the background of Figure 3.

1.3 Events

Each event has a name and a reaction (the body of the event) and belongs to an object. The name specifies the condition of the event, for example onClick – meaning that the mouse has clicked the object. The reaction of an event is a list of Logo instructions. When run by IMAGINE, it behaves in a similar manner to running a procedure with no inputs. Specifying events is a powerful way to incrementally build the behaviour of our microworlds. Although there are many standard events, the following are especially useful when developing microworlds with visualized math concepts:

- onClick — if an object owns such event, its reaction specifies what should happen if we click it. It may, for example, jump to another position, change its pen colour, increase its pen width, turn right by 90 degrees, etc. If a page owns such event, its reaction can colour a certain region or create a new object at that position etc.;
- onLeftDown — this event analyses the interaction with mouse in more detail. If you click an object, you first press the left mouse button over an object, and then you may drag and finally release the button. onLeftDown event specifies what should happen during the first phase of clicking the object. In the IMAGINE mosaic microworld all four sample tiles to the left have onLeftDown event, which specifies that a copy (a clone) of itself should be created and should stay here as far as the clicked tile will be dragged away from here and placed somewhere within the mosaic;
- onDrag, onLeftUp, onChange, etc.

1.4 Object-oriented Structure

In Blaho and Kalas (2001) we analyzed the object-oriented challenge for Logo creators and Logo educators. We noticed that for more and more Logo educators it is increasingly appealing to present object features to children. Unlike adults, children have no previous experience with any other (non-object-oriented) paradigm, so no transition is needed for them. Many activities and computer games children play have a kind of "object spirit" where you start by composing the game space out of a library of elementary parts and behaviours. We showed children how to use their object to develop problem solving. The object-oriented metaphor keeps the project more transparent and well structured, whenever:

- you need many identical objects with identical behaviours which won't be modified while running the project. In such case, clones of a prototype or several prototypes can easily be created as shown in the angles in Figure 3;

– you need many similar objects with minor individual differences, which may evolve while running the project. In such case, it may prove useful to specify classes (families) of similar objects (instances). The complete behaviour of each object results from combining common parts with private pieces. Whenever a new instance of a class is created, it simply gets its shape, position, heading and other elements of its behaviour.

In many IMAGINE projects we make use of a full object-oriented metaphor for creating generators of objects with complex behaviour. Such generators (like a tool button for adding another match or adding a new fraction, a new circle or a new cog wheel) may help the user both in his/her exploring visible math and understanding an object approach to problem solving as well.

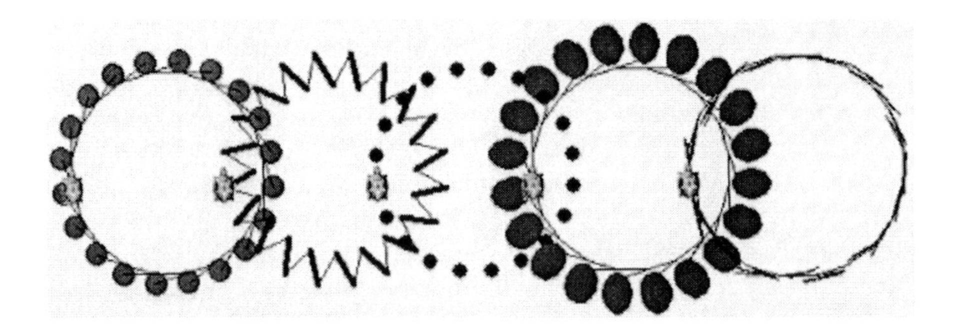

Figure 4. Five turtles above are drawing the same circle, each in its own way

Another powerful and useful object-oriented property is the possibility to make turtles interpret the same commands (even primitive ones) in different ways. Figure 4 illustrates how five turtles with the redefined fd command will draw a circle by repeat 20 [fd 20 rt 18]. The possibility to have private versions of any procedures may result in interesting effects like drawing in different symmetries, different transformations, sizes, colours, etc.

1.5 Parallel Processes

In IMAGINE we can launch several parallel processes. They run independently and can be used, for example, to:

– watch over relations and dependencies. In a dynamic geometry microworld, if we drag a point, there is probably a process (or several processes), which updates the shapes and positions of all dependant lines and circles. These changes themselves may trigger other processes to update objects;

- make objects regularly move forever, like planets rotating around a sun;
- make objects follow paths or curves described by lists of points or vectors;
- run various experiments, simulations, gadgets, dynamic models, etc.

1.6 Support From IMAGINE Data Structures

IMAGINE data structures (like lists of points [[x y] ...]) present powerful support for developers of educational applications (for math or other purposes). They are used for representing paths, lines, outlines or borders of areas. Even more flexible are lists of vectors, which are useful for transformations and computations with paths and curves.

2. SELECTION OF ACTIVITIES IN VISUAL MATH

Now we want to offer a selection of well-known visible math activities and match them to properties and techniques of IMAGINE, which makes it possible to implement them.

2.1 Constructing mosaics and exploring shapes

Regular shapes like squares, rectangles, triangles and other polygons, tiles, sticks, matches, cubes, etc. can be easily created by using programmable pictures. They will facilitate development of activities such as:

- Mosaics for exploring areas, symmetries and similarities. Tangrams and other activities/puzzles/games for exploring geometric shapes such as searching for all triangles/squares/polygons in a picture;
- 3-D mosaics, where pieces are identical cubes. They may be used for exploring volumes, building a structure by carrying out given instructions etc., exploring and understanding space.

When working with mosaics and shapes, we profit from automatic rotations of programmable pictures, an easy way to keep all pieces within a grid of regular points (either visible or hidden).

2.2 Exploring numbers, number sequences, using number rods and number lines, making use of different representations and visualizations of numbers

Programmable pictures may look like small cards with digits, numbers, signs of arithmetic operations, coins, bank notes, etc. In teaching/learning math, number rods or segments or figures of various heights are often used. In IMAGINE we can develop similar activities such as:

- Comparing, adding and sorting number rods according to their length;
- Experimenting on the number line. There may be cards with numbers attached to the line or certain animated characters, which can make steps to the left or right to visualize results of arithmetic operations.

When developing such activities in IMAGINE, we gain from direct manipulations like dragging and multiplying objects by cloning.

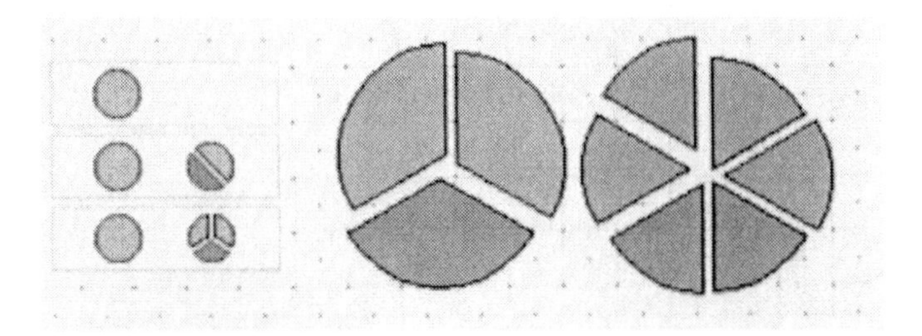

Figure 5. Playing with fractions: Dividing, comparing and adding

2.3 Exploring fractions

Figure 5 illustrates visual interactive environment for constructing, comparing and adding fractions.

2.4 Angles

Figure 3 illustrates an interactive environment for exploring angles. Each angle object is highly flexible. It can be dragged, rotated, increased, decreased or resized. It illustrates how powerful are objects (turtles) with programmable shapes and bright events.

2.5 Dynamic geometry

Probably the simplest shapes to create in Logo are points, segments, lines, circles, etc. And yet they present a surprisingly powerful tool and wide room for interesting activities. Dynamic geometry offers a wide palette of problems to be solved from very simple ones to rather complex ones such as:
– Exploring various kinds of symmetries, transformations and similarities;
– exploring distances, perimeters and lengths of borders of various shapes;
– solving simple planar constructions using points, lines and circles.

When such activities are being developed in IMAGINE, we deeply rely on events like onDrag, which repeatedly triggers recalculation and redrawing of all dependant objects. The object-oriented metaphor helps to keep the project transparent (with classes of objects like Circle, Point, Line, etc.).

2.6 Experimenting with combinations, statistics and probability

Learners are often expected to construct all possible combinations and permutations, and only later they encounter corresponding mathematical formulas. In IMAGINE any turtle can be assigned any bitmap as its shape. Combining this option with programmable shapes, we can build various basic elements for activities with combinations and permutations.

When exploring elementary statistics and probability in IMAGINE, we extensively make use of repeated computations and parallel processes for running simulations and experiments. While running them, the project records certain values and visualizes them instantly in one or another way.

2.7 Solving and constructing puzzles and labyrinths

Thanks to programmable shapes we can build pieces of certain mechanisms. The task is to combine several pieces into a functional unit. An example is the cogwheel microworld, where the final behaviour depends on the number of cogs of each wheel and the way we combine them. Programmable shapes and parallel processes are very helpful here.

There are many famous and popular puzzles in mathematics in which the task is either to move pieces respecting certain rules (e.g., game 15) or join pieces together so that they form certain shape (e.g., Pentamino). In this group of activities we should also mention mazes and labyrinths (2-D or 3-D) in which we usually have to find the shortest path or all possible paths, etc. When developing the activities in IMAGINE, we profit from the ease with which we rotate programmable shapes of objects and drag them.

2.8 Measuring, comparing and estimating

Another rich pool of activities originates from comparing, sorting, measuring, arranging and rearranging. Children can:

- sort pieces or any objects into groups of related things (based on their shapes, colours, size, meaning or functionality);
- explore and compare graphs of mathematical functions;
- experiment with a traditional watch with hands (adding or subtracting hours, halves and quarters of hours, minutes, study angles between hands, etc.).

Beside programmable shapes, parallel processes are broadly used when developing such activities in IMAGINE.

3. CONSIDERATIONS

Obviously, mathematical objects can be visualized and explored in different environments such as Visual Basic, Delphi, etc. However IMAGINE offers properties remarkably helpful for educational purposes:

- A rich environment for wide spectrum of users from learners of preschool age to the creators of educational materials and professional educational applications is provided. Very young children are already able to play with turtles, the very same turtles which are used to visualize complex math concepts.
- Turtle geometry offers well appreciated and elegant means to cope with graphical information.
- IMAGINE (Logo) projects are always open for further development and modifications.
- It is possible to assign either simple or very complex behaviour to its predefined actor/multiple actors (i.e., turtles). Also, we can assign simple or complex visualizations to turtles, still or animated.
- IMAGINE offers many modern programming features such as parallel processes, objects, events, communication through Internet, multimedia, etc.
- Logo itself has a long tradition in education.

When developing IMAGINE itself in previous years, its authors were inspired by Noss' (1997) vision of powerful computational systems which offer novel kinds of symbolism and innovative ways to manipulate mathematical objects. We hope that the result will encourage math teachers and developers to create new visible math educational materials.

REFERENCES

Blaho, A. and Kalas, I. (1998) Young students and future teachers as passengers on the Logo engine. In D. Tinsley and D. Johnson (eds.) *Information and Communications Technologies in School Mathematics. Proceedings of the IFIP WG3.1 Conference.* Grenoble. London: Chapman and Hall.

Blaho, A. and Kalas, I. (2001) Object Metaphor Helps Create Simple Logo Projects. *Proceedings of the 8th EuroLogo Conference.* Linz. Wien: Osterreichische Computer Gesellschaft.

Blaho, A., Kalas, I. and Matusova, M. (1994) Environment for Environments: New Metaphor for Logo. In D. Benzie and J. Wright (eds.) *Exploring a New Partnership: Children, Teachers and Technology. Proceedings of the IFIP WG3.5 Conference.* Philadelphia, PA. Amsterdam: North-Holland.

Kalas, I. and Blaho, A. (2000) IMAGINE... New generation of Logo: Programmable pictures. In D. Benzie and D. Passey (eds.) *Educational Uses of Information and Communication Technologies.Proceedings of the IFIP World Computer Congress.* Beijing, China. 427 – 430.

Noss, R. (1997) New Cultures, New Numeracies. An Inaugural Lecture. Institute of Education, University of London.

Watt, D. (1983) *Learning with Logo.* New York: McGraw-Hill.

BIOGRAPHIES

Ivan Kalas is an associate professor at Comenius University, Bratislava. He is a member of the steering committee of the national Slovak InfoAge project, which has already integrated more than 800 schools in Slovakia. Ivan is the head of the Department of Informatics Education, which is responsible for preservice education of teachers. He is author or co-author of several books and textbooks. Ivan represents Slovakia in IFIP TC3 Committee for education. He has presented papers at dozens of international conferences and workshops. In 2000 he worked as visiting researcher at the Institute of Education in London. He is a member of several international editorial boards and a member of program committees of several national, European and international conferences. He has read several invited lectures in UK, Brazil, USA, Hungary, Poland, Bulgaria, Czech republic and Portugal. He is a member of IFIP's Working Group 3.5.

Andrej Blaho is a senior lecturer at Comenius University where he gives lectures on introductory and advanced programming. He has taken part in several major national and international projects developing interactive educational computer environments for children and students. He is the author or co-author of several books and textbooks. His books on problem solving received the Publisher's Awards in 1991 and in 1999. He is a member of IFIP's Working Group 3.5.

Ivan and Andrej wrote *SuperLogo: Learning by Developing*, which was published by Logotron, UK in 1998 and has been translated into two other languages. They developed several educational software environments, which are being used in more than 20 countries. The tools aim at developing creativity, logical and algorithmic thinking, communication and co-operation. Together with Peter Tomcsanyi they developed SuperLogo and, in 2001, together with Lubo Salanci, they released IMAGINE, a new generation computer tool for education.

Cooperative networks enable shared knowledge

Rapid dissemination of innovative ideas and digital culture

Kate Crawford
Novae Research Group, Australian Technology Park, Eveleigh NSW, 1340, Australia; kate@novaeresearch.org

Abstract: The paper reports developmental research using Information and Communication Technologies (ICT) in support of the sharing of knowledge and expertise of digital culture. In both sites for advanced learning, cooperative team projects provide a way for stakeholders to exchange knowledge and become enabled by new technologies. Professional development provides advanced teacher knowledge on learning, motivation and engagement in problem-based learning as a basis for the use of hand-held computers and networks to support strategic cooperative thinking among teams. The skills and confidence of young students using networked ICT is shared with less technically confident teachers. Expert teacher design of the learning context continually draws students' attention to the kinds of capabilities, knowledge, thinking and tools that are used to achieve different goals.

Networked learning also has high economic value. A networked community comprised of teachers, students, scientists, and business people was developed to enable advanced learning in innovation. Three key features of the research projects were: The younger members of the community had the greatest knowledge of and commitment to communication and knowledge building in a digital culture; the development of authentic cooperation required all members to adopt new roles and rethink the traditional patterns of behaviour; teachers have made a particularly valuable professional contribution as they applied their expertise to facilitate learning and relationships for knowledge exchange.

Key Words: sites of learning, roles and relationships, professional development, collaboration, networks

1. INTRODUCTION: LEARNING AND INNOVATION

Innovation has until recently been conceived (and funded) largely in terms of scientific invention and related technical development. In most developed countries innovation has been largely confined to the "hard" sciences and kept one step removed from social considerations at least until commercial applications of the inventions are developed. Ignoring the surrounding cultural activity seems a serious oversight. Technical artefacts reflect the conditions of their production and the societies in which they are used — they have value because of the problems they solve and competitive or social advantages they give to particular groups of users. As Latour (1996) writes eloquently, people create their technical artefacts and are shaped by them in an intricate and continuous cycle. He explains:

> For the thing we are looking for is not a human being, nor is it an inhuman thing. It offers rather, a continuous passage, commerce, an interchange between what humans inscribe in it and what it prescribes to humans. It translates the one into the other. This thing is the non-human version of people; it is the human version of things, twice displaced.

Because of the intricate connection between people and tools, a successful innovation always perturbs, or places tensions on, the social relationships around it. This effect is particularly evident in well-established institutions with clearly defined power relationships and largely ritualised practices such as schools and universities. Educational institutions have been valued in the past for their stability and independence from social change. However, those are the very characteristics that now create tensions and make innovation difficult.

Despite wide acceptance of the need for reform in education, most new technologies have been under-used, ignored or resisted by educators. Good examples include: Logo programming developments by the MIT Media Lab and later Lego-Logo robotic devices, Genscope (BBN Labs and Concord Consortium), Tabletop (TERC) and Boxer (Andy DiSessa at U.C. Berkeley).

However new convergent information and communication technologies have never been appropriated so eagerly or used so enthusiastically and skilfully by young people· A recent survey at a major university found up to 80 percent of full-time university students working 20 hours or more per week. A common reason given for working was to fund Internet and mobile phone costs.

The emerging dynamics have resulted in a growing disjunction between:

- The social organisation and the use of technical applications in educational institutions.

– Their emerging impact on the knowledge, awareness and skills of young people in the wider community.

Young people are gaining skills and capabilities outside school at faster rate than their resistant elders who have traditionally played the role of experts. The two projects that are discussed below are seeking to find ways to harness the skills, enthusiasm, and new capabilities of young people, and encourage them to cooperate with others in the community in the process of inventing their future.

2. SOME THEORETICAL CONSIDERATIONS

Until recently, little attention has been paid to the dynamic processes of the evolving new "socio-technological" contexts in which many people live and work as well as their impact on human awareness, knowledge and capabilities. The new tools and the way we use them form an important new element in cultural experience and thus shape peoples' awareness, knowledge and capabilities. The impact of the new experiences is greatest for those people who, for developmental, access or other reasons, are most able to learn. They are usually young people. The emerging context presents the greatest challenges for older people who are carrying out roles that make learning, risk taking and experimentation difficult. In schools, teachers often feel as though they are in the latter group.

Activity theory is based on the idea that human activity is a dialectic relationship between subject (person) and object (purpose or goal). The perceived "object", or goal, of an Activity is, according to activity theorists (Engestrom 1999; Davydov 1991; Leont'ev 1981), *subjective* and distinct from its observable outcomes. People subordinate their thinking according to their subjective and often idiosyncratic interpretations of the purpose and potential strategic opportunities of Activity regardless of any organisational rationale for a task. Activity is comprised of actions (creative new responses) and operations (routine and well known habitual cognitive or behavioural processes, now commonly the domain of ICT systems), and also involves serious *intent*. The capitalised term "Activity" has been used to denote the purposeful forms of meaningful human activity involving both creative new actions and routine operations as described in the theory.

Each well-established community or organization has a complex set of shared and interrelated values, relationships, rules and roles that constitute a system of activity that is commonly mediated by specialized tools. Activity theory provides a useful framework to explain the relationships between:

– People and what they know, and their history of becoming knowledgeable.

– Their perceived/imagined interpretations of the possibilities for action in any context.
– The ways that Activity is mediated by the tools that are available.
– The role of people's personal intentions in shaping Activity.
– The rules, roles and responsibilities of institutional contexts and other communities that provide opportunities or constraints.

New kinds of collective capability and new forms of social organization, arising out of the wider use of ICT systems, have the potential to make it possible to design new contexts for learning, knowledge making and innovative Activities. In those new contexts, the rules, roles, responsibilities, and division of labour associated with learning in schools are reshaped according to the relative capabilities of the stakeholders that use them and the ways the new tools mediate the Activity and shape observable outcomes.

2.1 Learning and technology exchanges

In the first project, professional development for teachers was provided through intensive workshops to explore the implications of new technologies for the nature of knowledge and learning in the 21st century. It has become clear in the rest of the community, in developed countries, that machines now reproduce existing information and routine procedures that continue to be an important part of schooling. It has become clear that the traditional definitions of learning and knowledge in education need to be revised if the new technologies used by the rest of the community are to have a place in schools.

The project represents a cooperative venture between teachers, technology developers and educational researchers. It follows from earlier research that indicated that teachers had much greater difficulty using new technologies than young children, and that teacher knowledge about learning was tacit and rather narrow. The project had three elements. A research team collected data on observable teaching styles and their explanations for the Activity before and after an intensive professional development experience for participants. The professional development provided teachers with experiences in using new technologies (hand-held computers, networks and electronic measuring probes in Science), and also extensive input and opportunities to discuss and reflect together about:

- The new opportunities for learning and knowing that are emerging as a result of widespread use of ICT and new specialized technologies.
- The need to make those new thinking and learning activities explicit in school.
- The ways that roles and rules and division of labour shape the ways students think and learn.

The participating teachers, from three schools, were supplied with class sets of hand-held computers, electronic probes that could be operated attached to the mini-PCs, and new curriculum tasks that they had helped to prepare.

The teachers then returned to their classes and, despite a time lag between the course and when the new materials became available, began to experiment with new possibilities. Predictably, secondary teachers felt more constrained than elementary teachers, and younger children were more confident in using new technologies than older, adolescent students.

The following scenario in a middle school provides some indication of the kinds of observable outcomes that have emerged:

> The teacher, Marie (name supplied), has spent considerable time with her Year 7 class to explore and make explicit a wide range of patterns of thinking, knowing and cooperating with others. Everyone in the room has a well-developed understanding of the rules of the community and the kinds of Activity that are expected. The patterns of thinking, feeling and acting that they are using or have used are named and illustrated graphically on the walls of the classroom. They include such tactics as taking the role of an opponent in an argument to develop understanding of their perspectives and strategies. Students also critically analysed arguments presented verbally or in text. The students work cooperatively in teams and most of the time. The intranet and software at the school are used as tools to enable those kinds of activities. It has been repositioned as a tool for learning and for promoting and maintaining a high level of meta-cognitive awareness. In this classroom, most routine, repetitive processes are carried out by machines. Marie has some expertise in running the intranet but it is the children who have become authoritative about developing multimedia presentations and websites at the school.
>
> At 3.30 pm the bell rings, they pack up their project work and several from one team move to a classroom further on. The students are on roster to help others in the school learn to develop multimedia reports in a regular after-school class. They assume the role of tutors and advisors to a class that includes three teachers, one parent and several younger children. They are patient, courteous and very responsible in carrying out the community responsibility on a voluntary basis. Marie attends the class in a supervisory role and uses the time to make changes to the intranet. The Year 7 students share their knowledge and capabilities with the others in the room. After a few minutes one can be heard explaining patiently:

> You have to work it out for yourself but it's OK to watch others and ask questions. I'm here to help you learn to make your own project, not to tell you what to do. (Year 7 School 3)

A critical element in the project is the cooperative nature of the venture and the evolving new, and often blurred, roles and responsibilities for teachers and students. The successful use of the new technologies is emerging as a bi-product of the changing nature and purposes of the learning Activity. In particular, the new tools, and the facility and enthusiasm with which younger students use them, are being harnessed alongside the wisdom and emerging expertise of teachers about the design of learning contexts. An emerging role for teachers is as a learning coach — continually drawing the students' attention to the kinds of capabilities, knowledge, thinking and tools that are used to achieve goals that they have chosen. The new emphasis on metacognition (more conscious awareness and personal responsibility for intentions, goals and the choices of strategic Activity) places students in a new position as members of a community with new knowledge to share. It also ensures that they pay attention to and value new skills that they will need as adults. A new role for teachers is to create authentic opportunities and experiences for meaningful problem-based learning. A new challenge has emerged for both students and their teachers. Authentic problem solving using new tools often develops unexpected results. The knowledge, skills and confidence of young students using networked ICT are shared with less technically confident teachers, adults and younger children. In this field they are the acknowledged experts with a responsible role in the community.

2.2 Applications of networked learning to support technical innovation

New forms of networked learning have very high economic value. ICT is being used to address the needs of the emerging Australian photonics industry. In electronics the basic unit is the electron, in photonics the basic unit is a photon or particle of light. Optical fibres used in telecommunications are a common application of the emerging science. The new industry needs to recruit up to 20 000 suitably qualified people as researchers, developers, entrepreneurial business people and technicians for advanced manufacturing by 2010 to maintain its current share of the market in photonics. The field is at the same stage of development as electronics was 30 years ago and represents an important infrastructure technology for broadband networks and other applications requiring high speed signalling.

In the Photonics outreach program, students, scientists, business developers, teachers, technologists, and museum staff have joined an online "community of interest" that meets for community events, workshops and online work. By the end of 2002 the program will have reached more than 100 000 students. Young people, in middle school grades, play a vital role in the community that reflects their commitment to networked learning along with capabilities to develop skill and enthusiasm for networked technologies. Students with specialist knowledge from universities and technical colleges, and interested students from schools are currently cooperating to design an interactive web site that forms the focus for the community in the role of technical support and advice for other people in the community. They are developing interesting and intriguing activities in photonics, including games, puzzles and information design, based on recent scientific papers, for younger students. For teachers, developing new strategies for designing and managing e-learning contexts and working in cooperation with their students and also scientists and business developers represents an opportunity to explore the new possibilities for advanced learning.

2.3 Discussion

The two projects have both been built on earlier work investigating patterns of ICT use in knowledge intensive communities (Crawford and Crawford 1997; Hasan 2000) and the dynamics of constructionist learning online (Crawford and Crawford 2001). The two projects differ in scope and aim but share three key elements with earlier work:

- The younger members of the community had the greatest knowledge of and commitment to communication and knowledge building in a digital culture. Their contribution to the knowledge exchange is a critical element of both communities.
- The development of authentic cooperation required all members to adopt new roles and rethink the traditional patterns of behaviour, division of labour and relationships associated with transmission models of learning.
- The new teaching role in these ICT-enabled contexts was to:
- Make explicit and encourage the new processes of learning through meaningful and highly engaging activity;
- Facilitate the new, more direct, relationships between people who need to learn and those who have experience and knowledge.

It is becoming clear that new ICT-enabled virtual contexts for human activity are rich and complex, and potentially extend the scope of awareness and creative capabilities in ways that have not been possible before. The emerging evidence in the second project is that the new interactive and convergent technologies also have the potential to mediate cooperative activity that is inclusive of people who are members of normally disparate communities.

REFERENCES

Crawford, K. and Crawford, S. (1997) *Agency, Technology, and Vision: The Dynamics of Learning*, Sydney: The University of Sydney.

Crawford, K. and Crawford, S. (2001) School's Out. *HR Monthly* July 2001 28-29.

Davydov, V. V. (1991) The content and unsolved problems of Activity Theory. *Multidisciplinary Newsletter on Activity Theory* 7/8 1-35.

Engestrom, Y. (1999) Expansive visibilization of work: An Activity Theoretical perspective. *Computer Supported Work* 8 63-93.

Hasan, H. (2000) The mediating role of technology in making sense of information in a knowledge intensive industry. *Knowledge and Process Management* 6/2 72-82.

Latour, B. (1996) *Aramis or the Love of Technology. (Catherine Porter trans.) Cambridge, MA:* Harvard University Press.

Leon'tev, A.N. (1981) *Problems of the Development of the Mind*. Moscow: Progress.

BIOGRAPHY

Kate Crawford currently heads the Novae Research Group at the Australian Technology Park and works as a consultant with leading innovators to facilitate the entrepreneurial learning, knowledge making and development processes that are an essential element of technical and scientific innovation. She has designed and researched interactive networked environments to support learning, communication and cooperative innovation projects between previously disparate groups of people. Her research is based on grounded theories to explain the dynamics of human activity associated with scientific and technical innovation and the related development and design of institutional conditions to support entrepreneurial learning, research and development in rapidly changing new fields. She currently supervises research students from four universities.

Part Two

Teaching

Developing an ICT capability for learning

Steve Kennewell
University of Wales Swansea, Department of Education, Hendrefoelan, Swansea SA2 7NB, UK
s.e.kennewell@swan.ac.uk

Abstract: Learning effectively with Information and Communication Technology (ICT) requires an appropriate level of ICT capability. This paper explores the ways in which children develop their capability in home and school, and how their skills support ICT activity and learning in each setting. Conditions for developing ICT capability during such activities are identified using a framework for analysing learning situations based on affordances, constraints and abilities. It is concluded that all aspects of young children's ICT capability can be developed effectively through a combination of structured activities in school designed primarily for learning other subjects, provided that subsequent reflective activity is generated. This learning is supported by unstructured activities at home, and provided that they have access to appropriate guidance from more capable family and friends. Suggestions are made concerning the coordination of school and home ICT activities in order to exploit the positive features of each setting, and generate effective learning within and beyond the formal curriculum.

Key words: elementary education, conditions for learning, organising for learning, sites of learning

1. INTRODUCTION

Evaluations of the role of ICT in learning must consider different perspectives (Squires and MacDougall 1994) and recognise that the influence of ICT is dependent on the ICT capability of the user (Kennewell 2001). What the user knows about ICT affects the quality and quantity of the learning with ICT. The features of ICT that aid learning include interactivity and provisionality (Teacher Training Agency 1998). But to exploit interactivity, the user must know how to respond to screen prompts from the software; in order to exploit provisionality, the user must know how to save, load and edit work in progress. If learners do not have sufficient skills in using ICT, they experience the 'ICT interference factor' (Birnbaum 1990), and ICT becomes a barrier rather than an aid to learning.

The ability to use ICT to carry out worthwhile activity, including the learning of subjects other than ICT, has been characterised as ICT Capability (Kennewell, et al. 2000). Five key components of ICT capability have been identified:

- routines such as using a mouse or double clicking on an application;
- techniques such as adjusting margins to make text fit a page;
- key concepts such as menu, file, database, spreadsheet, web site or hypertext link;
- processes such as developing a presentation, seeking information, organising, analysing and presenting the results of a survey;
- higher-order skills and knowledge such as recognising when the use of ICT might be appropriate, planning how to approach a problem, making and testing hypotheses, monitoring progress in a task, evaluating the result, and reflecting on the effect of using ICT in a particular situation. (Kennewell, et al. 2000)

It is anticipated that those skills will develop together during the course of worthwhile tasks across increasingly challenging contexts, with help from those who are more capable.

2. INFLUENCE OF ICT ON LEARNING

Learning of specific subject matter is expected to take place through goal-directed activity in which there is a gap between the learning objectives and the student's current knowledge. The "learning gap" is bridged through cognitive effort. The learners utilise the affordances and constraints of the setting, such as those provided by ICT, in combination with their existing abilities in the subject matter to be learned, and in generic skills such as ICT capability. Those abilities, together with the affordances and constraints of the setting, provide both potential and structure for activity (Kennewell 2001). For example, when children are learning about the process of volcano eruption, they may use an encyclopaedia on a CD-ROM. The software affords searching by keyword and by successive focusing on subject headings; it also constrains the user to the specific material that the authors have decided to include. This constraint may be very valuable in the case of encyclopaedias designed especially for young children, although over time it will be unhelpful for children seeking up-to-date information. The CD-ROM does not do all the work and the child must know something about the process of searching and the particular techniques needed to carry out the searches with the CD-ROM. Furthermore, merely accessing information may not bring about learning and a reflective stage is an important element of the learning activity (Kennewell 2000).

The information retrieval scenario described above could take place in either home or school. The technological, human and cultural resources will vary between the formal school setting and the more informal setting of home. However, we may expect the differences in the features of the settings to have fundamental effects on the nature and process of children's learning with ICT. Home ICT activity is characterised by "bricolage" and "hard fun" (Papert 1996), whereas school use is largely routine, unstimulating (Kennewell, et al. 2000) and prescriptive (Sutherland, et al. 2000a).

3. FEATURES OF THE HOME SETTING

In the UK, the technological resources available in homes are increasingly sophisticated and widespread (Harrison, et. al. 2001). Indeed, many homes contain more sophisticated resources than schools (Kennewell, et al. 2000; Downes 1998), affording more effective presentation and access to greater range of information sources. Other affordances arise from the human and cultural resources available to support activity; for instance, the willingness and ability of parents and other family members to help, their networks of social and professional contacts, and the models of ICT activity that they provide (Sutherland, et al. 2000b).

Children's use of the resources may be constrained in various ways (Sutherland, et al. 2000b; Downes 1998). Table 1 illustrates some of the technological, human and cultural features that constrain home ICT use for children; some may have a positive effect on learning, others are potentially negative.

Table 1. Constraints on home use of ICT

Constraint	Example
Location of resources	In a communal room
Preparation needed	Connecting a telephone line for Internet connection
Parental restriction or security provision	Password protection on Internet filtering
Competition of hierarchy with family	Older siblings have priority
Perceived role in relation to technology	Feeling of inadequacy in comparison to more expert members of the family
Imposed priorities for different activities	School has priority over games

4. FEATURES OF THE SCHOOL SETTING

In school, different features are evident. First, the technology is usually based on a network, which affords the sharing of resources created for specific curriculum needs, access to a greater range of specific software and the exchange of ideas between pupils.

Second, the human support is of a professional nature. Many primary schools have appointed a specialist teacher for ICT, and most others have a coordinator for ICT who supports generalist class teachers by helping to produce plans for pupils' progression, schemes of work for each year and tasks designed to promote specific learning objectives. In the classroom, pupils often work in mixed ability pairs, seek help from their friends and "class experts", and increasingly, technicians and classroom assistants provide support for ICT activity (Kennewell, et al. 2000).

Third, the cultural resources are more communal in nature and specific to the planned curriculum. The effect of a whole class working on the same activity is valued by pupils (Kennewell 1993). The teacher expects that pupils will develop their work beyond their initial attempts. The practice of displaying children's work on the classroom and corridor walls, and the more recent adoption of electronic presentations affords the publishing of children's knowledge for the class or even a wider audience.

There are different constraints, too. Some may have a negative effect: School software may be unfamiliar to pupils with expertise developed at home, network crashes may mean computers are unavailable at times, some teachers may not give pupils access to resources which they have not been taught to use. Other constraints are designed to have a positive effect through providing structure for children's learning, such as limiting the time spent on enhancing presentation, focusing Internet use on specific educational web sites, and creating a rota to ensure that all pupils' access to computers is regular and systematic. The requirement to explain to a "less able" peer can also have a positive effect on children's concept formation.

The most significant feature of the school setting, however, is the role of the teacher in setting differentiated tasks that have an appropriate learning gap within a carefully planned curriculum, then orchestrating the affordances and constraints of ICT in a manner that is contingent on pupils' existing and developing abilities, and finally promoting reflection on the activity.

In primary schools in the UK, it is common practice for an ICT task to be introduced to the whole class. Pairs of pupils then work on the activity using one or more computers in the classroom on a rota basis over a number of days. When all children have worked on the task, a whole class plenary session is held in order to question pupils about their work, evaluate their learning, focus their attention on the concepts and skills developed, and discuss other applications of the ideas. Furthermore, the teacher will normally plan the ICT task and plan the teacher input to develop the children's knowledge in other curriculum areas as well as developing ICT capability (Kennewell, et al. 2000).

5. GOALS AND THE MONITORING OF PROGRESS

Another major difference between the home and the school setting is in the nature of the goals. At home, the goals are largely those of the children, despite the use of "school work" as an argument for acquiring the computer in many cases (Sutherland, et al. 2001b); at school, the goals are largely those of the teacher.

Children view learning using computers at home as a much more pleasant activity than learning from teachers in school. Pupils with computers at home often indicate that they are far more independent in their learning (Kennewell, et al. 2000) and have time for exploration (Sutherland, et al. 2000a). But that independence has implications for learning, both about ICT and with ICT. When there is a learning gap to be bridged, some cognitive effort is required; the child's reaction to the situation is crucial.

There are a number of possible reactions to difficulties in using ICT to solve problems which children have demonstrated in various contexts:
- give up and pursue another activity;
- use an alternative strategy which is inefficient but known to achieve the desired effect;
- ask a more expert child;
- ask an adult (parent, teacher, technician, classroom assistant);
- use the "Help" function;
- consult a printed guide. (Kennewell 2002; Sutherland, et al. 2000a)

Some of the strategies are likely to result in learning, but some will clearly not do so, and for others their effectiveness will depend on how well the support provided matches the ability of the child. In the classroom setting, we can expect the teacher to monitor task progress and the achievement of learning objectives. That approach is not without its problems, since many teachers have not yet developed a high level of expertise in evaluating ICT-based learning, but the children should at least recognise a certain expectation on the part of the teacher and feel accountable for their efforts. In the home, that accountability is largely absent and whether the children learn from their experience depends a lot on their self-regulatory abilities. The locus of control, represented by the choice of activity, time of engagement and depth of study, has a significant effect on motivation, concentration and perseverance. The trial-and-error approach, characteristic of home activity, may therefore be successful in achieving an outcome for the task. This is a weak strategy for solving problems, however, and, without a reflective stage, it is likely that little will have been learned either in ICT or in the context in which it is applied. The development of metacognitive knowledge and skills are essential to the application of cognitive knowledge and skills in a setting different from that in which they were developed, and discussion of a problem-solving strategy is important in fostering metacognition (Tanner and Jones 1994). There is some evidence that such talk occurs at home (Monteith 1998), but unfortunately schools often require too little planning, monitoring, decision making and evaluation of work from pupils (Kennewell, et al. 2000).

6. CONCLUSION

If children's ICT capability is to develop rapidly in the early years of schooling so as to aid learning from activities across the curriculum, it is clearly sensible for approaches to ICT use in school and home to be coordinated as far as possible. There is little point in trying to make them identical; rather, the features of each setting that enhance learning should be developed and a liaison fostered in order to produce a whole greater than the sum of the parts.

Children do not tend to make links between their activities in home and school without help. Teachers should try to replicate the conditions of "hard fun": viz. a large learning gap, with unfamiliar constraints but high levels of affordance. They should also recognise the inefficiency of "bricolage" — a wide range of routines but an incomplete range of techniques and limited knowledge of processes — and help children to develop and apply more formal knowledge of ICT through direct teaching and reflective activity. Finally, they should promote and develop metacognitive skills so that children can better regulate their home ICT activity themselves. Parents should continue to provide time for exploration and help with using efficient techniques, while providing helpful constraints in the form of expectations for learning with ICT, rather than merely imposing restrictions on ICT use.

REFERENCES

Birnbaum, I. (1990) The assessment of IT capability. *Journal of Computer Assisted Learning* 6 88-97.

Downes, T. (1998) Using the computer at home. In M. Monteith (ed.) *IT for Learning Enhancement* 61-78. Exeter: Intellect.

Harrison, C., Fisher, T., Haw, K., Lewin, C., Mavers, D., Scrimshaw, P. and Somekh, B. (2001) *ImpacT2: Emerging Findings from the Evaluation of the Impact of Information and Communication Technologies on Pupil Attainment.* London: DfES

Kennewell, S. (1993) *Changes in Strategies for Teaching and Learning Across Primary/Secondary Transfer.* Swansea: University of Wales Swansea.

Kennewell, S. (2001) Using affordances and constraints to evaluate the use of ICT in teaching and learning. *Journal of Information Technology and Teacher Education* 10 101-116.

Kennewell, S. (2002) Good practice in teaching ICT as a subject at Key Stage 4. Coventry: Unpublished report to BECTA.

Kennewell, S., Parkinson, J. and Tanner, H. (2000) *Developing the ICT Capable School.* London: RoutledgeFalmer.

Monteith, M. (1998) The place of learning. In M. Monteith (ed.) *IT for Learning Enhancement* 61-78. Exeter: Intellect.

Papert, S. (1996) *The Connected Family: Bridging the Digital Generation Gap.* Atlanta, GA: Longstreet Press.

Squires, D. and McDougall, A. (1996) Software evaluation: A situated approach, *Journal of Computer Assisted Learning* 12 146-161.

Sutherland, R., Facer, K., Furlong, R., and Furlong, J. (2000a) SCREEN PLAY: An exploratory study of children's techno-popular culture. Report to the Economic and Social Science Research Council. http://www.bris.ac.uk/Depts/Education/fullresultsabbreviated.doc.

Sutherland, R., Facer, K., Furlong, R., and Furlong, J. (2000b) A new environment for education? The computer in the home. *Computers and Education* 34 195-212.

Tanner, H. F. R. and Jones, S. A. (1994) Using peer and self assessment to develop modelling skills with students aged 11 to 16: A socio-constructive view. *Educational Studies in Mathematics* 27 4 413-431.

Teacher Training Agency (1998) *The Use of ICT in Subject Teaching: Expected Outcomes for Teachers.* London: Teacher Training Agency and the Departments of Education.

BIOGRAPHY

Steve Kennewell is a former mathematics and ICT teacher. He leads an initial teacher education course in ICT as a specialist subject and is director of the taught graduate studies programme in the Department of Education, University of Wales Swansea. He is the editor of *Computer Education* and has jointly written two books concerning developing ICT capability and teaching ICT as a subject. He is a member of IFIP's Working Group 3.5.

Separated by a common technology? Factors affecting ICT-related activity in home and school

David Benzie
College of St Mark & St John, Derrifird Road, Plymouth PL6 8BH, UK; David_Benzie@compuserve.com

Abstract: There has been a steady growth in the number of computers in both home and school over the last decade and it is now clear that there is the potential for activities in those settings to be linked through a common technology.

This paper explores the relationship between computer-based activities in home and school by considering each of those settings as a distinct, but related, community of practice. The exploration of the relationship is based on Benzie's (2000) research that highlights the significance of power, motivation and legitimacy as forces which affect, in Lave and Wenger's (1991) terms, peripheral participation in a community of practice. The paper suggests that this perspective can be used to help shape worthwhile Information and Communication Technology (ICT)-related activities that link home and school.

Key words: social contexts, conditions for learning, sites of learning, organising for learning, roles and relationships

1. INTRODUCTION

There has been steady growth in the number of computers in homes and schools over the last decade. In the UK, by 1999 about 75 percent of children aged 7-11 claimed to have a computer at home (BECTa 2001a) and in primary schools the average computer-to-pupil ratio stood at 11:8 (DfES 2001). Given that a growing proportion of computers in both settings have an Internet connection and are PC compatibles running Microsoft Windows, it is clear that there is considerable scope for activities in those settings to be linked with the computer acting either as a platform to support similar activities in both contexts or as a mediator for communication between the two. BECTa's (2001b) report on the use of ICT to support home-school links, based on case studies in eight schools, highlights the early stage of developments in those institutions and also draws attention to the nature of their activities. As has been the case with other technology-related innovations in education, early concerns are with the technology itself (in this case, network infrastructures and web servers) and with using the technology to replicate and extend, as opposed to radically transform, current practice.

The pattern is hardly surprising but projects that seek to build worthwhile links between home and school need to take account of the social complexities in the two settings and the differences between them, that are richly illustrated in reports by Downes (1999), Facer, et al. (2001), McNamara, et al. (2000), Sanger, et al. (1997) and (2001a). Benzie's (2000) study of the development of student IT capability, written from the perspective of Lave and Wenger's (1991) and Wenger's (1998) theories concerning Communities of Practice, addresses a setting with features that resonate with the authors' reports despite its focus on adult and emerging adult learners. Two questions follow from Benzie's (2000) study. Firstly, "What are the messages concerning the relationship between ICT-related activities in one context and those in another?" Secondly, "What messages are there for those who seek to create ICT supported home-school links?" The questions are addressed in this paper.

2. THE DEVELOPMENT OF IT CAPABILITY: AN EXAMPLE OF ACTIVITY IN MULTIPLE CONTEXTS

Benzie (2000) studied the development of students' IT capability over a period of two and a half years whilst they completed undergraduate degrees. About half of the students were trainee teachers. In almost all cases the students developed their IT capability in multiple contexts, home, college and school were the most significant; but other contexts, such as church and the work place, also featured. The exploration of activity in those settings, using Wenger's (1998) perspectives on Communities of Practice, led to a number of significant conclusions.

The first conclusion was that different settings could be seen as separate but connected Communities of Practice. Individuals were almost invariably members of multiple communities (e.g., trainee teachers were part of a college community and, whilst on teaching practice, a school community), and they played a key role in linking practice. They "brokered", to use

Wenger's (1998) terminology, between different communities. However in spite of patterns of multiple membership, it was clear that conceptions of ICT capability varied between communities. In other words, ICT capability is a situated concept that only acquires meaning when referenced to a context.

The second conclusion concerned the identity of a learner. It was clear that the students in the study were active agents whose actions shaped and were shaped by the communities to which they belonged. In other words, there is a mutually constitutive relationship between the two. The relationship was neatly illustrated by a student who introduced new ideas into one of his teaching practice schools whilst his conception of good classroom practice shifted as he moved from one school to another.

A third conclusion concerned the manner in which individual engagement in a community of practice is shaped. Benzie (2000) concluded that engagement in community activity is shaped by the resulting force from three web-like structures, "Power", "Motivation" and "Legitimacy" as shown in Figure 1.

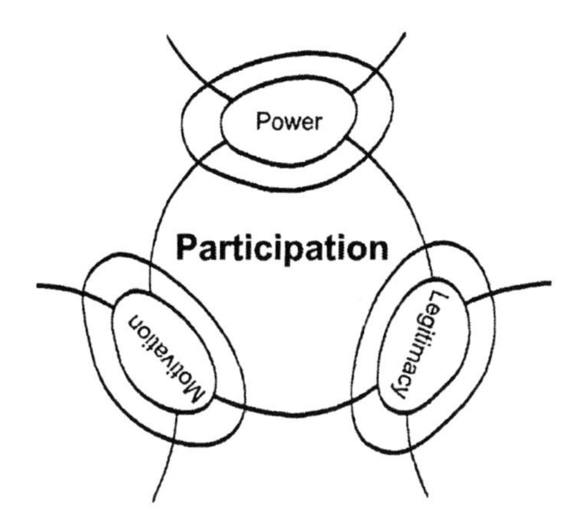

Figure 1. Patterns of participation and the webs of power, motivation and legitimacy. (Benzie 2000)

In order to engage in community activity an individual has to negotiate a set of power relationships with other members of the community who control access to the resources that are required. An individual's ability to conduct the negotiations can be affected by circumstances in other communities to which they belong. In the case of students there is, for example, an advantage that comes from having the funds to buy books and equipment that they perceive they need for enjoyment or professional development.

The motivational forces that affect participation in a community are complex. Lave and Wenger (1991) distinguish between "Use value" (e.g., "I can make direct use of the product of participation to enable me to achieve Y") and "Exchange value" (e.g., "If I gain qualification X, I can exchange it for a position in community Z"). The distinction draws attention to the way in which engagement in one community influences motivation to engage in another. Students in Benzie's (2000) study navigated interconnecting webs of motivating forces, linked to their membership of multiple communities, as they approached new activities.

The third web concerns the way in which specific activities are deemed legitimate. Communities draw distinctions between what is, and is not, a legitimate activity. A significant part of the story of becoming a member of a specific community is learning to appropriate and deploy the rationales which legitimate and promote some forms of activity in preference to others. However the legitimising rationales that individuals create for a specific activity are inevitably drawn, in part, from the other communities to which they belong. This can be very significant. For example, some students are, or have been, members of communities where play is not seen as a legitimate adult activity; rather, play is equated with time wasting. This can have disastrous consequences when the student seeks to participate in a community, such as many ICT-related communities, where "playful" activities are particularly effective.

Participation in one community can influence participation in another. The significance of this is illustrated by Wenger's (1998) suggestion that the role of education is to place "students on an outbound trajectory toward a broad field of possible identities." Peripheral participation leading to an outbound trajectory with multiple connections and outcomes can be seen in Figure 2.

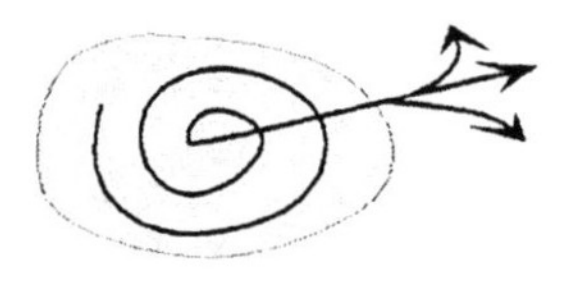

Figure 2. Peripheral participation in an academic community of practice leading to a broad field of possible identities. (Benzie 2000)

The figure illustrates the multiple trajectories and also suggests a dynamic in which a successful educational community promotes "peripheral participation", a positive term from Lave and Wenger's lexicon, in the activities that it legitimates. The quality of peripheral participation in an educational community may be judged by the effectiveness with which students are prepared for roles in other communities. Special attention should be paid to the role that an educational community has in enabling students to develop identities that are characterised by their negotiability in other contexts.

Benzie (2000) suggests that there are a number of characteristics of a higher education community that enable its learners to develop negotiable identities.

A successful community:

- continuously renegotiates the meaning and significance of the objects and conceptual frameworks that are associated with its activities;
- organises the peripheral participation of students in ways that expose the canonical meaning and significance of community objects and frameworks to them whilst also enabling them to negotiate specific meanings, linking those objects and frameworks to activity in other communities of which they are a member;
- ensures that student participation is periodically scrutinised by lecturers — the purpose of scrutiny is to maintain peripheral as opposed to marginal patterns of participation;
- encourages students to play emerging master roles in their interactions with peers; peripheral participation is associated with moves towards symmetrical relationships;
- places a high value on activities associated with exploration and reflection, both should occur within the frame of contemporary community activity and at the boundary with other communities;
- regards the giving and receiving of help as particularly significant activities;
- provides, maintains and grants access to the physical resources that are required to facilitate participation.

Home and school can also be seen as communities of practice so the message from the research for those who seek to initiate ICT supported home-school links will now be considered.

3. ICT AND HOME-SCHOOL LINKS: SOME SUGGESTIONS

When the development of identity is fundamentally linked to educational aims, as illustrated in Figure 2, activity may be tested by the question, "Is the activity structured in a way that allows children to develop identities that are negotiable in a broad range of contexts beyond school?" The word "structure" is a heavily loaded one for it carries the baggage of the sociocultural context in which activity takes place. Focusing discussion about ICT and home-school links around the concepts of power, motivation and legitimacy helps to keep these issues in the foreground.

3.1 Power

It is all too easy to reduce issues of power to one of domestic finance. Any attempt to use ICT to support home-school links will have to consider the availability of computers, software and network services in the home but this should not be the only consideration.

Research by Downes (1999) suggests that when computers are available in a home children have little difficulty in negotiating access in order to enable them to complete school-related tasks as those tasks are generally given a high priority. What is significant is who exercises the power to dictate the nature of the school-related activities. If children are not allowed to play a part in shaping them they will simply maintain and reinforce the asymmetrical power relationship that generally exists between adult and child.

There is a second sting. If parents and teachers retain control of all aspects of activity that link home and school they will surely use the technology to increase their surveillance of children. Home-school e-mails will focus on what the child, as a third party, is (or is not) doing as he or she trudges towards a goal that s/he has played no part in choosing. The lure of automated registration systems that allow parents to check their child's attendance at each and every lesson, simply by logging on to the school web site, will be irresistible even though the reality is that only a small proportion of children really need their attendance to be closely monitored. Such a use of technology to subjugate children may have outcomes that are the very opposite of the ones that are desired.

Children's activities do need to be scrutinised by adults but the purpose of scrutiny is not to dominate and subjugate. Rather, it is to uncover misunderstandings and misconceptions in ways that help barriers to progress to be removed. For teachers and parents, the process of scrutiny should help to illuminate differences between home and school conceptions of activity in a way that can then lead to renegotiation and an increased degree of alignment between the two.

The tendency to subjugate can be countered by allowing children to have some say in the determination of activities that underpin home-school links. There would be at least two significant benefits from this. Firstly, children would be highly likely to base some of their suggestions on their experiences in communities beyond home and school, so activities associated with home-school would play a positive role in helping them to negotiate positions in those communities. The second benefit is that allowing children to play a part in shaping activity creates a channel through which parents and teachers can become more aware of the nature of activities that children choose to engage in. Teachers may not see this as a benefit because of the challenge that it presents to traditional school-directed activity but the alternative is a growing gulf between activity in home and school.

3.2 Motivation

Effective home-school links will only be created and maintained if teachers, parents and children all have a stake in their success. McNamara, et al. (2000) say that knowing that their child is "doing OK" is the central concern for many parents. It is clear that computer technology can provide a channel for relatively straightforward communication on the subject. Many parents also want help to enable them to support their children with homework and they frequently miss the paper-based information that is erratically conveyed from home to school in children's bags. There are some obvious ICT-related solutions to those issues, though the solutions are based on the assumption that technology is available in the home and that the culture in the home is supportive of the school and its aims.

Superficially, children are motivated to engage in an activity by its immediate, as opposed to its long term, value. For this reason, generalised appeals to "develop life skills", for example, are likely to be futile. Adults generally convert long-term educational objectives for children into a series of short-term ones such as grade achievement. Attempts to motivate children to engage in activity (e.g., home use of online revision materials) by creating a link with the achievement of better grades at school will be heavily mediated by the home perspective on achievement at school.

An alternative approach is for schools to seek to stimulate activities in the home that have an immediate value, possibly in terms of enhanced status, to the child either in the context of home or in a context beyond home and school. Encouraging children to look for ICT tractable problems in the home, or in other social groups to which they belong, and then to devise and implement solutions to those problems is just one way in which this might be done. This gives the added virtue of creating a channel through which homes can influence school.

Attempts to motivate teachers are always going to face difficulties in contexts where they are assessed according to their ability to guide children through national tests that are structured in ways that promote a view of legitimate activity that differs widely from the view of legitimacy that exits in many homes. The flow of ideas from home to school is likely to complicate the traditional patterns of a teacher's day-to-day practices as the messages associated with those ideas will not fit in comfortably with other pressures. Current structures in education encourage teachers to see ICT mediated home-school links as largely uni-directional, and as an agent through which power and control are exerted. Such a perspective will only be countered if teachers can be motivated to hear, and act on, the messages that flow back to school. Constructing joint enterprises between home and school, in which both have a stake, is one way in which this could happen.

3.3 Legitimacy

A key aspect of the difference between home and school concerns the conception of legitimate uses for technology. Parents in many homes willingly legitimate school-related activity but there are also some significant cultural barriers between school and many homes. Children, for example, inhabit an electronic world where the wholesale swapping and sharing of electronic resources (especially music and, increasingly, video) is seen as entirely legitimate. This is at odds with notions of legitimacy that schools are required to promote.

The legitimacy, or otherwise, of ways of working is also an issue. Exploration and "fiddling around" are, for example, effective learning strategies that many young children use quite naturally. However they are not always legitimated at school or in some homes. In the long run social pressures lead many children to de-legitimise them. Schools seeking to build effective ICT-mediated home-school links need to consider the legitimacy that is accorded in each context to the ways of working that are implicit in any proposed activity.

The availability of help in each context for activity is critical and the way in which it is provided reflects a perspective on legitimate activity. If, for example, completion of a task by any available means is seen as legitimate, it is likely that children will seek help in ways that actually hinder their long-term progress, as when children develop a private economy in which they complete homework for each other. There are some delicate issues here because children do need to learn to play emerging master roles with their peers and one way they can do this is to become a source of help for each other.

4. CONCLUDING REMARKS

Research by Downes (2000), Facer, et al. (2001) and Sanger, et al. (1997) highlights the dislocation that exists between the home and school ICT-related tasks that many children engage in. There are, however, many good reasons for wanting to build more effective links between home and school, and ICT has created new ways in which this can happen.

Effective links depend on far more than technology. Building links will present a challenge to cultures in both home and school as dislocations between the two contexts are grappled with. A vocabulary to support the discussion, and a perspective on the nature of the challenges, can be generated by considering two contexts as communities of practice. When children are seen as active agents who participate in the activities of multiple communities, attention is drawn to the web-like forces of power, motivation and legitimacy with which they engage. They traverse the webs in their own way, but their patterns of engagement in community activity are nonetheless shaped by webs that draw threads from each community to which they belong. School and home are, for most children, but two of the communities in which they are involved. Awareness of the role of power, motivation and legitimacy in home-to-school connections can be used to help design home-school links that liberate, rather than subjugate, children.

REFERENCES

BECTa (2001a). *ImpaCT2: Emerging Findings from the Evaluation of the Impact of Information and Communication Technologies on Pupil Attainment.* London: DfES http://www.becta.org.uk/impact2.

BECTa (2001b). *Using ICT to Enhance Home-school links. An Evaluation of Current Practice in England.* London: DfES http://www.becta.org.uk/homeschoollinks.

Benzie, D.H. (2000) A longitudinal study of the development of information technology capability by students in an institute of higher education. Unpublished Ph.D. thesis. Exeter: University of Exeter. David_Benzie@compuserve.com.

DfES (2001). *Survey of Information and Communications Technology in Schools 2001.* National Statistics Bulletin Issue No 09/01 October 2001. London: HMSO.

Downes, T. (1999) Playing with computing technologies in the home. *Education and Information Technologies* 4 1 65-79.

Facer, K., Sutherland, R., Furlong, R. and Furlong, J. (2001) What's the point of using computers? The development of young people's computer expertise in the home. *New Media & Society* 3 2 199-219.

Lave, J. and Wenger, E. (1991) *Situated Learning. Legitimate Peripheral Participation.* Cambridge: Cambridge University Press.

McNamara, O., Hustler, D., Stronach, I., Rodrigo, M., Beresford, E. and Botcherby, S. (2000) Room to manoeuvre: mobilising the 'active partner' in home-school relations. *British Educational Research Journal* 26 4 473-489.

Sanger, J., Willson, J., Davies, B. and Whittaker, R. (1997) *Young Children, Videos and Computer Games. Issues for Teachers and Parents.* London: Falmer Press.

Wenger, E. (1998) *Communities of Practice. Learning, Meaning, and Identity.* Cambridge: Cambridge University Press.

BIOGRAPHY

David Benzie is the Director of the Centre for Information Technology in Education (CITE) at the College of St Mark & St John. He teaches a wide range of courses, including those that focus on in-service and pre-service training for teachers. His research is concerned with socio-cultural theories of learning and the contribution that they can make to the design of learning environments. He is a member of IFIP's Working Group 3.5.

The interaction between primary teachers' perceptions of ICT and their pedagogy

Avril M. Loveless
School of Education, University of Brighton, Falmer, Brighton, BN1 9PH, UK; aml@brighton.ac.ukalmer, Brighton

Abstract: A qualitative, case study approach was used to investigate the perceptions and pedagogy of a small group of teachers working within one school, Carberry Junior School in England. The study was carried out during an eighteen-month period of significant change in primary schools responding to the UK Government's National Grid for Learning (NGfL) initiative and its impact on models of access to ICT resources and expectations in teaching and pupil achievement. The paper highlights the teachers' perceptions of Information and Communication Technology (ICT) as a social and cultural phenomenon, as an ambiguous area constructed as a discrete subject, curriculum resource and higher-order capability, and as a "new" field in primary schools. An interactive model is proposed to describe the interaction of the teachers' perceptions and pedagogy. The case study can offer insight to a consideration of professional development with ICT in primary schools during a period of rapid change in resource provision and expectations of teachers' use of ICT to support teaching and learning.

Key words: elementary education, social contexts, research, professional development, change

1. INTRODUCTION

Teachers of young children engage with new information and communication technologies within wide social and cultural contexts. In the United Kingdom they work with a range of ambiguous constructions of subject knowledge of ICT capability that underpin educational policy expressed in the National Curriculum, and expectations of teacher training and professional development. A case study was conducted in an English

Junior School at a time of transition and change. The UK initiative for the National Grid for Learning provided opportunities for new models of access to ICT resources within the school, and raised expectations of teachers' competence and confidence in the use of ICT to support subject teaching. The analysis focused on the interaction between perceptions of ICT and pedagogy as an expression of dimensions of professional knowledge.

2. THE CONTEXTS FOR THE STUDY

2.1 Social and cultural contexts

The social and cultural contexts in which ICT resources are perceived and used by teachers are key influences in the development of a range of personal and professional practices. Anxieties are expressed about new visions of the post-industrial society, how we learn to adapt to new labour patterns in our society, and how ICT can be used for controlling information, surveillance, marketing, and invasions of privacy. There are wider and often contradictory underlying perceptions of technology in contemporary Western society in two dominant paradigms of technological and social determinism. The debates form a backdrop to the development and expression of teachers' perceptions of the role of ICT in their professional work.

2.2 Perspectives on ICT capability

A concept of "ICT capability" is central to teachers' work within the framework of the Statutory National Curriculum which underpins planning, coordination and presentation of the curriculum, assessment and pupils' achievements (Department for Education and Employment 1999). The term is ambiguous in government curriculum policy, reflecting different and developing aims and intentions. Given some of the ambiguities and changes in definition and focus of ICT capability, it is difficult to predict primary teachers' perceptions of ICT capability and its role in learning.

2.3 Teachers' perceptions and beliefs about ICT

A study of the influence of teachers' perceptions and beliefs about ICT in their practice identifies two types of approaches: (1) the computer awareness approach that recognises the ubiquity of ICT in wider society and (2) the pedagogic approach that uses ICT to facilitate teaching and learning objectives (Drenoyianni and Selwood 1998). The majority of the teachers questioned indicated a computer awareness approach, and even some of those teachers expressing a pedagogic approach demonstrated discrepancies between their statements and their classroom practice. That practice focused on computer skills rather than integrated learning intentions. Changes in practice often related more to issues of management and organisation than to learning and assessment objectives. The study raises questions about what created and reinforced the beliefs that underlie different practices and the possible confusion in official documentation and guidance, indicating a lack of consensus and understanding of a conceptual framework for ICT in education.

Teachers' perceptions of ICT in education are not only influenced by official documents and guidelines, but also by their own experiences of using ICT for personal reasons in a social and professional context where the profile of and access to ICT resources is fast-changing. Dawes' study (1999) investigating key factors enabling teachers to acquire "network literacy" identified, not a model of teacher deficit and resistance, but a pragmatic approach to change as the new ICT resources were being incorporated into school practice

2.4 Models of professional knowledge

Descriptions and discussions of pedagogy as an expression of teachers' professional knowledge have developed in both breadth and subtlety, acknowledging developments in understandings of the contexts and content of learning and teaching (Watkins and Mortimore 1999). The strands of subject knowledge, pedagogical representation, personal beliefs and values, and the context of situated learning are woven together into a dynamic and interactive model of teacher professional knowledge proposed by Banks, Leach and Moon (1999). Teachers learn to be teachers in situations that are relevant and authentic. A development of the model highlights the interactions between subject knowledge, pedagogical content knowledge, pedagogic knowledge, identity and community that are held in tension by the teachers' experiences of, and reflections upon, change in their practice (Loveless 2001).

3. RESEARCH METHODOLOGY

At Carberry Junior School (CJS), the teachers taught all aspects of the National Curriculum to children aged 7 to 11 years (Key Stage 2). Inspection reports described the children attending the school as presenting an "average" profile, demonstrating the full range of attainments expected for that Key Stage. The quality of teaching in the school was described as "high" by local education authority advisors. There was a positive ethos in school development, an innovative approach to the development of ICT in the school and an open attitude to involvement in research.

The research methods used to explore the teachers' perceptions of ICT and pedagogical practices used the ethnographic techniques of in-depth interviews with teachers, observation of classroom practice, narrative descriptions and use of written material such as school documentation. The study presented an analysis of the teachers' perceptions and professional knowledge.

4. TEACHERS' PERCEPTIONS OF ICT

"Perceptions of ICT" was grouped into three sub-themes: Perceptions of ICT in society, perceptions of ICT capability and perceptions of ICT in schools.

4.1 Perceptions of ICT: Its impact on society

The Information Society was portrayed as inevitable and pervasive, focused on economic and social change, and closely associated with issues of participation in the future development of society. As well as descriptions of the future involving excitement, change, opportunity and progress, the teachers also presented images of the "Information Society" as sources of anxiety and concern. They expressed the need to "keep up" with the cultural phenomena of irrevocability and rapid change. They tended to accept the view of children's "inherent computer capabilities" without critique, and discussed their general concerns about entitlement, equity and their professional responsibilities towards equipping the children for the future. Concerns about access to computers and information for "haves and have nots" were expressed.

The children's access to ICT at home was a significant issue and the school was seen as playing an important role in providing equal access to the facilities. No detailed discussion of the types of experiences that children might have with ICT out of school, nor the implications of literacy, culture and content described by commentators on the "Digital Divide" occurred.

Concern emerged about the demands placed upon teachers to keep up with the changes in technology, and the children's understanding and use. Another issue was the expectation for teachers to deliver a curriculum that would equip children for the future.

Three teachers used phrases such as: "We owe it to the children to give them a good start," and "You've got to overcome your own personal feelings and do it, otherwise you'll feel that you are short changing the children," and "They'd be at a huge disadvantage. The children are going to suffer. They are going to need it in life." Those expressions of the importance of ICT competence for the children's future participation, rather than their immediate learning needs, also echo those of parents and teachers in Downes study (1998).

4.2 Teachers' perceptions of ICT capability

Teachers' perceptions of ICT capability as "subject" or "tool" or "capability" were not clearly distinguished and should not be considered as mutually exclusive categories. The confusion and ambiguity were admitted openly and the teachers described their attempts to weave the strands together to make connections between ICT as a discrete subject and a cross-curricular tool. Teachers perceived the importance of teaching the children to acquire the skills for using ICT resources. The need for younger children to be well grounded in skills was reinforced and the discrete nature of the direct teaching of skills and techniques was also described.

Closely linked was the perception of ICT as a distinct subject domain given priority in curriculum policy and resource provision. One teacher emphatically said, "It's also a tool for all the others (curriculum areas), but you can't use it effectively as a tool for the others until you have learned it as a subject in its own right."

ICT was likened to music or physical education, subjects that required the teacher to have "specialist" knowledge, skills and understanding. ICT capability as a subject was not viewed as a collection of discrete skills, techniques and processes. Teachers perceived ways ICT could be embedded in the context of other subjects and used as a tool to support learning and teaching.

Some curriculum subjects were considered to be more appropriately supported by ICT than others, although there was little consensus about what these might be! In trying to explain the experience of perceiving ICT as a subject and a tool in the curriculum, one of the teachers summarised the issue that she felt she faced in dealing with the two perspectives in her own practice:

> It's a lot easier to teach it as a subject, just like using the skills that you have to do but it's a lot more fun when they see where it links in.

4.3 Teachers' perceptions of ICT in schools

After thirty years of government ICT strategies, teachers described the application of ICT in the primary school as "new" and "rapidly changing". Teachers' resistance and resilience to technological change has been vividly described by a number of researchers and commentators (Selwyn 1999). But other researchers describe teachers' pragmatic reasons for not using new technologies: Motivation is low when classroom resources are limited, and the curriculum and assessment framework does not require high status/high stakes contributions of ICT (Watson 1997; Dawes 1999).

The NGfL provision of networked resources in schools and the requirement for ICT development plans contributed to perceptions of change in resources for teaching and learning. Teachers saw ICT as a new experience, unrelated to previous attempts to implement the National Curriculum for ICT. Their descriptions of ICT in schools as "new" and a "new subject" were related much more closely to their personal experiences of using ICT at home and in school in meaningful and successful ways than to the twelve years of National Curriculum Programmes of Study.

The teachers reported recent changes in their own use and attitudes when they had flexible access to ICT at appropriate times, usually at home. They recognised the increased access that the children had outside school. So perceptions of ICT in schools seemed to be influenced by the nature of the activities that ICT facilitated: Standardised applications, communications and whole class access (which were authentic in the teachers' own experience of planning, preparing and implementing relevant learning activities for the children).

The teachers' visions of how classrooms might change in the next ten years also gave insights into their perceptions of ICT in schools. Despite the predictions of classrooms without walls and the networked teacher engaging with knowledge and learners in different ways (Scrimshaw 1997), the future visions of the teachers were conservative. Their predictions of the effect of ICT on the nature of their work in the next ten years related to classrooms equipped with more resources rather than different models of interaction with learners and knowledge. Some expressed anxiety about a dystopian view of the future with technology balanced by a sceptical view of the resistance to change within the school system. One teacher considered that the "... side of teaching which is important is the social skills, having someone there to ask", and did not want to teach from home via a web site. Her colleague was more concerned that change in schools would not reflect the potential of ICT for supporting new strategies for learning and teaching. She described her vision of "... lots and lots of activities. Things would be set up and the children would be more familiar with them and able to access things by themselves and get on by themselves, but then some classrooms I'm sure would be just the same!"

5. INTERACTIONS BETWEEN PRIMARY TEACHERS' PERCEPTIONS OF ICT AND THEIR PEDAGOGY

Perceptions of ICT are fashioned by the teachers' identity and participation in wider cultural and social spheres that influence the professional arenas and settings in which they practice. Their perceptions reflect the ongoing negotiations of meanings of ICT as they work with young children. As students and teachers reflect upon their constructions of ICT and their own knowledge, skills and understanding, it is important to encourage their awareness of the ambiguities and different perspectives in trying to define ICT. They need not see them as sources of anxiety but can learn to hold them in tension. They can develop a range of practices: A focus on techniques and applications; the use of ICT resources to support specific learning objectives; the development of higher-order thinking; collaboration and communication with the appropriate use of ICT tools and media.

Models of professional development need to recognise how teachers' perceptions of the purpose and potential of ICT are grounded in a sociocultural context. Current models of Initial Teacher Training and Continuing Professional Development for ICT are ostensibly linked to pedagogic practice, but often lack the sense of trajectory for teachers. Instead the models focus on evidence of competence rather than confidence in change, and do not draw upon a mutual interaction between experiences in home and school contexts. Developing confidence in the use of ICT is high stakes for those who regard it as an integral part of their identity as teachers with responsibilities for their pupils' short term achievement in statutory assessment and long term participation in an Information Society.

REFERENCES

Banks, F., Leach, J., and Moon, B. (1999) New understandings of teachers' pedagogic knowledge. In J. Leach and B. Moon (eds.) *Learners and Pedagogy.* London: Paul Chapman Publishing in association with The Open University Press.

Dawes, L. (1999) First connections: Teachers and the National Grid for Learning. *Computers and Education* 33 4 235 - 252.

Department for Education and Employment. (1999) *The National Curriculum for England: Information and Communication Technology.* London: DfEE.

Downes, T. (1998) Children's use of computers in their homes. Unpublished Ph.D. thesis. Sydney: University of Western Sidney.
Drenoyianni, H. and Selwood, I. D. (1998) Conceptions or misconceptions? Primary teachers' perceptions and use of computers in the classroom. *Education and Information Technologies* 3 87-99.
Loveless, A. M. (2001) The interaction between primary teachers' perceptions of information and communication technology (ICT) and pedagogy. Unpublished Ph.D. thesis. Brighton: University of Brighton.
Scrimshaw, P. (1997) *Computers and the teachers' role*. In B. Somekh and N. Davis (eds.) *Using Information Technology Effectively in Teaching and Learning*. London: Routledge.
Selwyn, N. (1999) Why the computer is not dominating schools: A failure of policy or a failure of practice? *Cambridge Journal of Education* 29 1 77 - 91.
Watkins, C. and Mortimore, P. (1999). Pedagogy: What do we know? In P. Mortimore (ed.) *Understanding Pedagogy and Its Impact on Learning*. London: Paul Chapman Publishing.
Watson, D. (1997) A dichotomy of purpose: The effect on teachers of government initiatives in Information Technology. In B. Samways and D. Passey (eds.) *IT Supporting Change through Teacher Education: Proceedings of the IFIP Joint Conference of Working Group 3.1 and 3.5, Israel*. London: Chapman & Hall.

BIOGRAPHY

Avril M. Loveless is a Principal Lecturer in ICT in Education at the University of Brighton, UK. She has published a number of books and articles relating to the use of ICT in learning and teaching, focusing on Primary Education. Her current research interests include pedagogy and ICT, and the creative use of digital technologies. She has been the chair of the Association for Information Technology in Teacher Education and is the currently the editor of the *Journal of IT for Teacher Education*. She is the chair of Creating Spaces, a network of independent professionals promoting creative uses of technology. She is a member of IFIP's Working Group 3.5.

Capacity building in tele-houses

A model for tele-mentoring

Márta Turcsányi-Szabó
Eötvös Loránd University, Informatics Methodology Group 1117 Budapest, Pázmány Péter Sétány 1C. Hungary; turcsanyine@ludens.elte.hu

Abstract: This paper describes the tele-house pilot project designed to serve Hungarian learning communities. In the project participating children are mentored by students in pre-service Informatics courses using distance learning technology. Two web-based learning material collections designed by the TEAM Lab <http://www.team-lab.ini.hu> provide a constructivist approach and allow different learning styles to emerge. The NETLogo component provides self-paced discovery learning with individual guidance while the Creative Communications component provides project-based group learning with collaboration and group mentoring. The pilot project went through two sessions of an Action Research process that aimed to build a suitable model extendable to the whole network of tele-houses and to contribute to the introduction of distance education in order to support under-developed regions of Hungary.

Key words: collaboration, social context, sites of learning, roles and relationships, teacher education

1. INTRODUCTION

A tele-house <http://www.telehaz.hu> is a multifunction Information and Communication Technology (ICT) service centre. Designed for small villages, the tele-house is "a community telecommunications service house", a physical entity that provides computer and office infrastructure, as well as instruction in organisational and mass communication issues for communities. The tele-house can be economically managed to serve a range of individuals, groups, small communities, and so serves many social needs. The first session was funded by USAID <www.telehaz.hu/hosted/page20>

and in the second year through an application to the Hungarian Prime Minister's Office for additional funding.

Tele-houses are expected to provide services directly applicable to any individual within the community, should evolve from local needs and can be accessed by anyone. The idea for tele-houses in Hungary emerged from active civil initiatives resulting in large scale projects. A year ago there were about 200 tele-houses in operation; at present the number has doubled. Since the government and several civil organisations realise their importance in the community and provide more funds now, the number will probably double soon.

Two questions arise immediately: "What role can a tele-house play to support local economic development, local organisation, services, connections between small and large regions, and emerging systems (e-business and working across distances, for example)?" and "How can a tele-house fulfil those tasks?" In response, we say that tele-houses play a key role in the development of a region by providing access to remote educational services.

To facilitate the process, the pilot project established a bond between the tele-house movement and the TEAM Lab, a university-based research group, in providing a suitable and extendable environment for capacity building in partly-isolated regions of Hungary. The project has passed through two Action Research sessions and has created a model of the learning situation that could be extended and further researched for improvements. The resulting spread of tele-houses can provide a widespread solution to problems of under-development and low-level resourcing. Our guiding research question not only asks, "Is it possible?" but also, "How and under what conditions is it possible to help capacity building by remote means in under-developed regions?"

2. THE SITUATION

Some parts of Hungary, especially the eastern part, are considered under-developed. Unemployment in some regions is over 70 percent and the infrastructure does not allow the emergence of new economies. In the under-developed regions education above elementary school level is provided only at nearby cities, and the only realistic dream of young and old is to find a "way out".

Local courses, with or without ICT provisions, provide only isolated remedies and spread very slowly. There is little possibility of those local courses spreading to other regions. Distance learning promises greater speed and more variety of themes with possible updates later on. But the culture leading to distance education needs to be accepted and practised in order to enable future progress in the right direction. The ultimate goal would be distance-based work, which would provide motivation for both the younger generation and their elders to remain in their regions and work via ICT-based initiatives.

Tele-houses could provide a virtual "way out" by remaining physically in the home region, allowing a "virtual view outside" the stagnant economic situation in which children live. The tele-houses could promote connections within and between regions, help people seek information and find economic possibilities. At present there is no clear strategy towards the right way of effecting large scale change but tele-houses can be part of a long-term solution.

Currently, tele-houses are open to all, but the services offered, as well as the cost of maintenance, must be considered as far as short- and long-range planning for under-developed regional support is concerned. The positive side of undecided policies results in open doors for all but there is no clear concept of what can happen next. Capacity building in an educational context can be one of the roles for tele-houses to provide, even though they are not conventional forms of education, yet the model could be extended to build a network for such development throughout Hungary.

3. PEDAGOGICAL FRAMEWORK

Our choice for the tele-houses as the scene of many activities is partly intentional. The sponsors aimed at starting up tele-house activities and children were already actively accessing tele-houses, so we began to give them meaningful activities that could add value to their use of ICT and further their growth in other subject areas. We thought that a non-school situation would help establish a non-compulsory and non-instructional environment where the local helper is not a professional on the subject but is also a learner himself/herself.

The nature a of tele-house implies the freedom of access on a community basis and not on the basis of being affiliated to a school by definition. So the tele-houses provide freedom to attend with friends and family members. That way the tele-houses take on the flavour of social engagement. We do believe that the same situation could be established in schools, especially in the form of an after-school activity club.

Our basic philosophy for the design of our pedagogical framework is to use the Logo philosophy. We use different authoring tools for multidisciplinary creations and self-expression. We want to involve children in playful learning to motivate them with the non-compulsory tasks that engage them in autonomous, self-paced learning. For this we provide a playful explorative environment so they can engage themselves with themes of their own liking.

Within the different themes we offer them convergent and divergent assignments for "learning by doing" in order to engage them in a more active role of progressive learning and creative expression (Turcsányi-Szabó 2000). We offer the children several tools and encourage them to express themselves in their own individual ways.

At the same time we also provide tools for more analytic, systematic and constructive thinking through games that interest them. The tools introduced in the learning environment are not only intended to determine "what" is to be learned. The expressive nature and the freedom of fulfilling the assignments indicates "why" they need to learn. The focus is not on learning tools but showing what is possible with the tools if one is persistent enough to keep on learning. That approach, in the long run, might give children ideas for future work.

The project aims to encourage "collaborative learning" in a community based on individual and group learning. A community-driven activity seems to be a realistic approach in case of tele-houses. It results in individual and collaborative learning with both online and offline activities, and enhances real-time communication. Since learning goals are aimed at the younger generation, it is highly recommended that the balance of activities emphasise real life collaboration with some necessary elements implemented online.

The transfer effect of such learning is intended to progress in two directions: Participants learn the way to work in a distance learning situation and the dissemination of knowledge gained can be communicated to the rest of the community. The learning materials provide both individual and project-based learning situations that apply in both learning and working situations. In some cases, when the younger generation first learns to be fluent with technology, knowledge is actually transferred by children to their parents and family in a natural and effective way.

4. EDUCATIONAL SETTING

The educational setting is based on the local environment as well as maintenance and support from the university-based central project site, the attitude of local helpers, the attitude of the distant mentors, the projected aims of developed web-based learning materials (WBL) — which will be described below — as well as the strategy used. The project is continuously monitored by researchers to provide evaluations and advice on necessary modifications between Action Research sessions.

4.1 Tele-houses

The tele-house project provides the necessary equipment, software tools, maintenance and supervision for the communitites' existing infrastructure. Tele-houses had to apply for the funds to provide a workable infrastructure from the start. The tele-houses operate from a tele-house centre with an e-Room <www.eroom.com> as common working space equipped with an e-mailing service.

The mentors are experts who have already mastered the WBL materials and mentoring methods, while local helpers are the ones responsible for local activities. Mentors have been chosen from fourth or fifth year pre-service Informatics students. The mentors' roles are to:

- visit their assigned tele-house as often as they can, a minimum of twice towards the beginning of the project;
- acquire a fairly good idea of the local situation, individual and group problems, and find ways to motivate children;
- maintain good contact with all children and local helpers;
- answer letters within 24 hours;
- guide each child individually on a path that suits best personal growth;
- always react and comment positively on submitted works and induce further progress;
- provide a fixed weekly slot where he/she is available for synchronous communication over the phone or network chat;
- provide continuous evaluation on each child's progress.

4.2 Design of WBL courseware

The two WBL materials, NETLogo and Creative Communications, were developed in the TEAM Lab at Eötvös Loránd University in Budapest and are designed to support both individual and collaborative project-based group learning. The materials enable capacity building of ICT skills through different applications, and allow for the exploration and development of multidisciplinary skills and creativity.

4.2.1 NETLogo

NETLogo is comprised of three parts. The first part is an objectivist Logo course leading learners step-by-step to master the Comenius Logo environment through context-driven tasks and assignments. The material should be user-driven, self-paced, and also coached by the local helper and/or distant mentor. The second part contains constructivist microworld modules dealing with different themes. Learners' individual interests and proficiency guide the children as they move through the Logo course. In both parts, each unit is divided into several streams.

The Summary stream describes the unit, the concepts, primitives of the Logo language and activities the children can engage in. The Task setting stream provides the children with several task assignments and processes for solutions. The Self-check stream provides questions or tests, and there are problems to be solved and submitted. The Self-check stream also provides a place for "Reflection", afterthoughts of the children once they have worked through the course (Turcsányi-Szabó 2000).

The WBL material includes a CD-ROM containing the Comenius Logo authoring tool (Turcsányi-Szabó 1997) and a beginner's book (Stuur and Turcsányi-Szabó 1998). Many subject microworlds have a connection with the Creative Communications activities to promote creative ideas, expressions and artistic works.

The third part of NETLogo contains guidance for teachers/mentors/helpers on how to coach learners to progress with microworld exploration and construction. It provides diverse starting points and links to allow different paths to be taken by learners. The different units offer methods for handling learning problems as they occur. The units also give tasks and projects that tele-house users must complete and submit. An analysis and evaluation of the implementation of material in different learning settings is also provided.

The basic aim of the material in the case of elementary school children is to help them master modelling as a basic tool for investigations that call for problem solving, building structures, debugging ideas and working in virtual environments.

The basic aim of the material in case of teachers (helpers) is to enable them to use and configure educational microworlds for children's needs, to be able to guide children through collaborative modelling practices, and be able to design simple microworlds for multidisciplinary use. NETLogo creates one type of learning environment and its complement, Creative Communications, solves the problem of helping children learn and use currently available software packages that they must master to compete both within and outside their regions.

4.2.2 Creative Communications

The Creative Communications component of the tele-house project is made up of two parts. The first part is a collection of courses that guide users in the use of the existing software tools — Microsoft Windows and Office, Internet Explorer, FrontPage, Macromedia Flash, Asymetrix Cool Edit, and Corel Print Office. Instruction is also provided on how to compose photos, how to retouch digital photos, how to design a presentation, how to search the Internet, Netiquette, etc. The material should be user-driven (depending on the themes to be tackled), self-paced, and coached by the local helper and/or distant mentor.

The second part of Creative Communications consists of several project units grouped according to themes such as writing, narration, typography, visual representation, montage, motion; and concept maps. Children must choose one theme but the concept maps unit is compulsory.

Each unit is divided into streams. There is an Introduction (with a description of the unit, concepts, and ideas for connecting thoughts). The Practice stream provides several exploratory tasks and ideas for expression within the theme. The Assignments stream gives assignments where the tele-house participant must create and submit materials s/he has produced.

The Self-check stream asks what new topics have been learned, what was interesting, problematic, boring, hard, easy, and what wishes the child might have for further assignments. The Reflection stream asks for afterthoughts once the projects have been completed. Project units can be worked on individually or through local collaboration, and have strict deadlines to allow the global processing of others' work in a next unit. The final unit requires the design and implementation of a presentation introducing the whole local group and should be done collaboratively to use knowledge mastered through progress within different themes.

The basic aim of the material in case of elementary school children is to enable them to integrate subject knowledge and ICT skills while promoting critical thinking and creative expression on an interdisciplinary platform. The process is based on self-motivation with the intention that the children will learn how to collaborate in real and virtual environments, and be able to fulfil deadlines.

The basic aim of the material in case of teachers (helpers) is to be able to explore ICT tools and their application on different tasks where the emphasis is not on the tool, but the process of creation itself. The teacher/helpers should also be able to integrate assignments with on- and off-computer activities to enhance the creative process. But learning to use tools expressively is only a partial aim. Learning to work with those tools in a group is an essential solution for under-developed regions in Hungary.

4.3 Group learning strategy

The group-based working method has the following characteristics:

- Choosing group size with a maximum of ten users took care of possible dropouts. Children visit tele-houses at one group slot time and several free

slots are available during the week. Thus children mainly work in pairs of two to three or, in some cases, a larger group where pairs often arise from originally existing friendships or family ties.
- Positive interdependence develops during work, emerging from the natural ties of everyday activities. Thus individual problems are first discussed on a peer level.
- Individual accountability is attained through the constant individual submission scheme proposed by the WBL material and the one-to-one communication with mentor, who occasionally provides additional individual tasks, though peer or small group work is preferred at times!
- Final group tasks must be a presentation that mirrors the fingerprints of all participants so that the efforts of individuals add up to group contribution. The Creative Communication WBL material even emphasises the additive nature by the compulsory choice of different themes.
- Local helpers are advised to act as coaches who facilitate constructivist learning that should take place in an autonomous "student-centred" manner based on self-pacing and individual motivation.

Tele-mentoring takes place on an individual level in case of the NETLogo material and on a group level in case of Creative Communications, while mentors continuously provide help for local helpers.

The visits of mentors to their assigned tele-house are crucial events that can determine the overall relationship of the individuals and group towards the mentor. The occasions should be used so the mentors and children get to know each other, develop confidence, establish personal relationship, and evoke the natural notion of wanting to progress further.

Mentors develop friendships with children by playing games in order to develop close relationships, not only for themselves, but to act as a team-building bond among the group itself. A four-day camping session, joining children from all tele-houses, was also realised after the first session. The real life events, games, and real communication have been the basic adhesives of community cohesion and resulted in further continuation via virtual ties between children and tele-house helpers.

4.4 Research method

Although the project was originally planned to last ten months — from September till June, the actual project lasted only during a six month session — December 2000 till June 2001 with a four-day camping event in July ending the session. That schedule allowed an in-between evaluation in March after which some changes could take place to adjust the problems arising within the Action Research session. The second session took place from September 2001 till December 2001. Portfolio analysis of the children's work generated during the session is still under way.

Data was collected from 70 children in five tele-houses taking part in the first session as well as from 150 children in 11 tele-houses. Four of the telehouses taking part in the second session were also present in the first session. We also collected data from an additional elementary and secondary school where the materials were allowed to be used freely depending on the teacher.

Researchers maintain an overview of the process and immediately take note of conditions and resulting experiences to add to their research assignments within the Action Research process to lead the project to success. The project co-ordinator, Marta Turcsányi-Szabó, keeps the whole project going, while the administrative organiser from the tele-house centre attends to local technical issues.

The project uses an inductive research strategy including:

- Separate descriptions are compiled by both local helpers and distant mentors about the local situation, the process applied to fulfil the project, the problems encountered, the progress achieved in case of each child or inability encountered with an explanation of possible reasons. Note is made of any positive or negative experiences in connection with the project.
- Pre- and post-written structured questionnaires enquire about individual situations and interests, subject knowledge in ICT, attitudes about using computers and the role of ICT in society. The questionnaires also assess attitudes, behaviour and motivation of children towards computer games, which is a separate research issue.
- A 30 minute IQ test assesses children's logical, visual, and problem solving abilities.
- A portfolio analysis of the submitted work of each learner in comparison to individual situation, abilities, basic knowledge, progress, achievements, test results, and degree of creativity provides information on what has been accomplished.

5. OUTCOMES

The pilot project did provide valuable feedback for future methods and tools needed. It also provided a possible model for e-learning in tele-houses using distant mentoring.

Our approach managed to accomplish the following goals:

- Children living in remote under-developed areas succeeded in mastering not only basic ICT skills, but also developed fluency in expressing

themselves with different tools and they learned the basics of learning at a distance.
- Children realised that computer games not only can be fun but that many opportunities are awaiting them through the use of ICT as they plan for their future.
- Student teachers tele-mentoring children's activities learned about the needs of children and the different methods and tools that can develop skills. They also learned how to motivate and evaluate, and learned about the different platforms of ICT use in everyday life and expression. The project made them understand the values and drawbacks of living in small remote communities and the ways capacity building can improve under-developed regions via ICT.

A few months after project closure, the following impacts can be seen:
- Tele-houses presented children with their certificates of participation at a town meeting, which increased the interest of the whole community in finding a way for continuation.
- One of the communities established an art school with media studies as a form of continuation where local artists could scaffold the skills of talented children.
- A physically impaired boy, who participated in both sessions, is now continuing his secondary studies at a distance.
- Surprisingly large numbers of participants choose Informatics themes in their secondary studies.
- Most children are confidently using e-mailing as a new form of social communication and were able to make good progress in an Internet Challenge game that we launched for schools.
- After project funding ended, we offered continuation of our mentoring, aiming at the ability to produce web pages introducing their local town and community. This ability opened the eyes of the locals to the tools and the possibilities of attracting outsiders to their region.
- Tele-houses in the most under-developed regions are more than grateful for the possibility, since, as they say, "It is not only our eyes that have been opened, but that of the world too, to see us."

It is now up to the tele-house movement as well as government sources to decide on any further continuation of tele-mentoring processes. In the wake of the outcomes, however, the participants are very hopeful that the process will have a continuation.

REFERENCES

Stuur, A. and Turcsányi-Szabó. M. (1998) *Comenius Logo játék és programozás. (Comenius Logo games and programming*) Budapest: Kossuth Publishing Ltd.

Turcsányi-Szabó, M. (1997) Hungarian Comenius Logo. Budapest: Kossuth Publishing Ltd.

Turcsányi-Szabó, M. (2000) Subject oriented microworld extendible environment for learning and tailoring educational tools: A scope for teacher training. In D. Benzie and D. Passey (eds.) *Proceedings of Conference on Educational Uses of Information and Communication technologies*. Beijing: China.

BIOGRAPHY

Márta Turcsányi-Szabó received a Ph.D. in mathematics (Informatics) and is an associate professor at the Eötvös Loránd University, Informatics Methodology Group. Her research field includes application systems, design principles of educational programs, and the integration of computers into the creative learning process. She is head of the TEAM lab which is involved in evaluation, research and development of educational multimedia tools. Marta is a member of IFIP's Working Group 3.5.

Part Three

Policy

ICT for rural education

A developing country perspective

Pedro Hepp and Ernesto Laval
Instituto de Informática Educativa, Universidad de La Frontera, Casilla 380, Temuco, Chile; phepp@iie.ufro.cl

Abstract: In 1991, as part of its educational reform, the Chilean government launched the Information and Communication Technologies (ICT) in Schools initiative, the "Enlaces Network". Its aim is to properly integrate ICT into Chilean public schools. After more than ten years of development, with 100 percent of Chilean secondary schools and more than 50 percent of the primary schools already using ICT, Enlaces is entering a new phase with a more curriculum-oriented focus and with the goal of incorporating all rural schools by year 2005.

The paper addresses the main implementation constraints of the Chilean rural environment and their effect on the ongoing ICT policy: The geographical isolation and precarious infrastructure; the fact that rural schools are usually very small schools with different grades sharing the same classroom. The cultural reality of rural areas involves a special kind of relationship between the school and the local community. Those constraints, together with the previous experience with Enlaces in different Chilean realities, have been taken into account to define a special ICT policy for rural schools in Chile. First, a special long-term teacher training program with a specific pedagogical approach that fits a rural environment has been developed and tested in pilot schools. Second, the definition of a local support organisation to help sustain development strategies in the long run has been established. Third, the hardware and software infrastructure required and Internet access have also been analysed together with the technical support. Finally, community involvement in school activities was also included in the policy.

Key words: elementary education, conditions for learning, developing countries

1. THE CHILEAN EDUCATIONAL REFORM

Chile is a country with close to 15 million inhabitants with a UNDP Human Development Index of 38 among 160 countries and 16 percent of the population is rural.

Its educational system has close to 10 300 schools (9 000 primary and 1 300 secondary schools), 130 000 teachers and 3 100 000 students (2 300 000 in primary and 800 000 in secondary schools). The rural population data are shown in Table 1.

Table 1. Chilean rural schools

Characteristics of rural schools	Number of schools
One teacher school	2115 (65%)
Less than twenty students per school	1600 (49%)
Regular public transportation	706 (22%)
Schools with electricity	3027 (92%)
Schools with telephones	653 (20%)
Total number of rural schools	3280 (100%)

For the last twelve years, Chile has undergone major educational reform. A new curriculum for both primary and secondary education has been designed and gradually introduced in all school grades; new teaching and learning methodologies are being implemented in order to achieve a higher quality and more equity in our education; more resources, textbooks, infrastructure and better teacher salaries are all part of the comprehensive effort. The Information Technology initiative, the "Enlaces Network", is an important component of the reform and aims to determine the benefits, contents, costs and replicability of initiatives involving educational computing and networking in Chilean public schools. It incorporates mechanisms for evaluating impact and seeks to determine the roles of computer technology on schools with the fewest resources (Hepp 1999).

In 2001, after 10 years of implementation, Enlaces could show the following results: three million students (90 percent) using ICT in 6 300 Schools (5 000 primary and all 1 300 Secondary); 70 000 teachers trained; 75 percent of all schools with free Internet; ICT is an integral part of the new curriculum; teachers have access to a special plan to buy low cost computers; and total expenditure of Enlaces for the decade US$110 Million.

Each school has received: Teacher training for three years together with technical support; equipment (38 000 computers together with printers, local area networks and furniture); a variety of productivity and educational software; free Internet access for most schools; and curriculum-oriented digital content on Internet. As a result, Chile has now 57 students/computer; 9/14 computers per primary/secondary school; and 10 teachers per computer.

In 2000, after completing its main goals, Enlaces began a new era and the rural schools became one of the highest priorities for the next six years. They were not included from the beginning because their poor infrastructure and weak communication facilities made it very difficult for Enlaces to train teachers and incorporate computers. After more than a decade of progress with the educational reform and improved conditions, Enlaces was ready to embrace rural education.

2. ICT FOR THE RURAL SCHOOLS

2.1 Institutional framework

Since its beginning, Enlaces has built a working relationship with close to 25 universities all over the country that contribute to the program with teacher training activities and materials, web-based content production, software evaluation, field research and healthy criticism. The universities are organized in five geographical zones for their work with Enlaces. The southern zone has the largest number of rural schools where piloting began a few years ago. The zone has 1 651 schools, about 50 percent of the total, with an average of 27 students and 1.6 teachers per school.

To improve the information exchange with the rural schools and also to promote the sharing of ideas and solutions among them, the Ministry of Education works on a monthly basis with groups of schools geographically close to one another organized in clusters of five to twelve schools per cluster. The clusters are called "microcenters" (San Miguel 1999; Wenger 1998). In the southern zone 1 651 schools have been grouped into 231 microcenters with an average of 7.1 schools per cluster.

Each university that works with Enlaces has the responsibility for a number of microcenters for a period of at least three years. Their work is closely coordinated with other professionals from the local Ministry of Education that attend the same schools and they normally organize together each visit to the microcenter meetings. Specially prepared teacher trainers attend each microcenter at least four times a year and visit a specific school another four times. Given the geographical situation of many of the schools, visits may last for a whole day and sometimes, during winter, even longer.

2.2 Rural Conditions and Opportunities

Chilean rural schools present a number of characteristics that are different from urban schools and call for a special ICT policy. The characteristics can be grouped in four categories: Location, infrastructure, size and culture. Although they offer new challenges for an ICT policy, some of the schools represent a unique opportunity for change and innovation inside a classroom.

2.2.1 Infrastructure

Most rural schools are small buildings comprising a single classroom, an office for the teacher and space to store material. Most of them have now stable electricity or will soon have thanks to a national initiative for all rural communities.

When schools have dial-up phone lines with low bandwidth, e-mail is provided during low fare periods of time using store-and-forward protocols through an ad-hoc software product developed by Enlaces: "La Plaza" (Hepp, Alvarez, Hinostroza and Laval 1993) as shown in Figure 1.

Figure 1. La Plaza: a user-friendly interface for primary schools

Although rural schools now have relatively good structures, normally wood with isolated walls and roofs, the schools' environmental conditions may negatively affect hardware, especially in schools that are close to the sea with its sand, salt and humidity, or amidst a windy and dusty countryside. Roads are normally without asphalt, and in windy and dry days the levels of dust will pose a real threat to moving parts in all equipment.

Those conditions call for a training strategy that includes basic technical skills for preventive and basic hardware maintenance to cope with the most common problems that arise in the ICT infrastructure of the school. The maintenance information has been gathered after many years of work with small schools, so Enlaces technical managers now provide a very specific set of problem-solving routines for all teachers and trainers.

When technical or economical conditions don't allow Internet access (Trucano and Hawkins 2002), the school receives a set of CD-ROMs with educational web sites that have been carefully selected and documented. The CD-ROMs are safe for students because of their selected content and students can use the software to communicate with other students as shown in Figure 2.

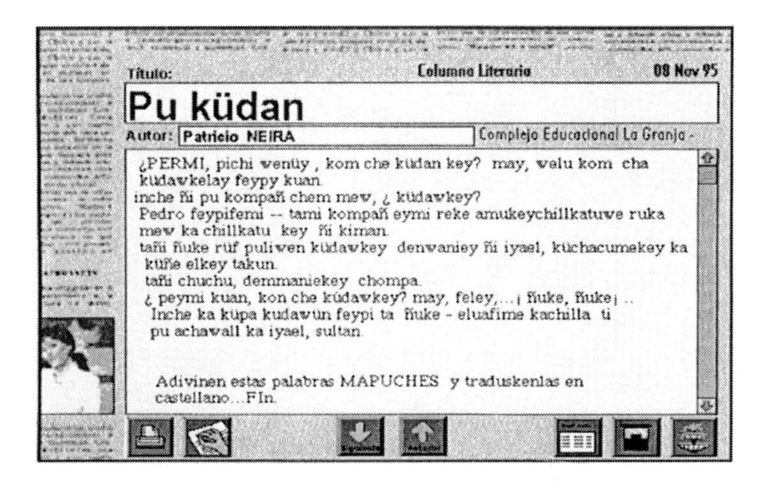

Figure 2. "Mapuche" e-mail written by an indigenous student using La Plaza

Such restricted Internet use allows rural students to have access to valuable content that is usually found on the Internet (such as literature, music, science, museums), but implies some restriction to the access of communication services and content based on online database access.

The Enlaces team is closely following new technical alternatives for rural communication (Trucano and Hawkins 2002; WorldLinks 2001) such as satellite connections but the alternatives require a high investment in infrastructure, making the service extremely expensive for a low number of access points. Use of a satellite segment still has a monthly cost of several thousand dollars but could be used to provide shared Internet access to thousands of schools. Each school would need an initial investment of less than US$10 000, but costs are becoming more affordable. The monthly fare would be less than US$50.

2.2.2 Location

Rural schools are normally located far from urban areas where technical assistance is more readily available. In many cases there is no local public transportation so teachers and students have to walk everyday from their houses to school, increasing transportation costs (e.g., delivery and maintenance of equipment and software, training activities and visits).

The long distances that are normally required to reach a rural school, restricted access in some places during the winter or particularly remote locations (i.e., schools in distant islands), require a teacher training and support strategy during concentrated periods of the year, another reason for the teachers to learn some basic hardware maintenance procedures. They should be capable of solving most hardware and software configuration problems by themselves. Achieving a relative autonomy from urban support centers is a goal of the training program.

2.2.3 Size

Most rural schools are located in areas with low population density so they are very small schools sharing the same classroom with different grades. The situation poses a number of challenges, but interestingly, it also offers new opportunities for outstanding learning situations using ICT.

One of the main challenges for teachers in rural schools is to provide a simultaneous pedagogical intervention with several grade levels in the same classroom. Small mixed-class schools offer a good opportunity for organizing the classroom in groups of similar learning levels. Also, conditions seem to offer a suitable opportunity for having the computer as a learning resource available for small-group collaborative work inside the classroom in a learning corner.

Collaborative-based learning (Campos, Cerda, Villarroel and Rivera 1998; Crook 1994) using ICT tools is one of the main strategies in rural environments. If Internet is available, the strategy may have the most profound effects in small and isolated schools where restricted conversation spaces around a few people do not offer the diversity of urban environments. With the Internet, collaborative projects may reach students from other schools in the same region and also students and teachers from all over the world, amplifying the quality of the conversational spaces and stimulating social interaction (Burniske and Monke 2001; Crook 1994; Githiora-Updike 2000). Chilean schools are stimulated to work on projects such as WorldLinks, I*EARN and Think.Com.

Small schools usually involve the challenge of a reduced number of teachers. In many cases, the lone teacher in a school might have a nonprofessional initial formation and also lack a professional support network. In those cases it is important to provide a peer support network, especially when facing a highly demanding cultural challenge like the one represented by the introduction of ICT. Teacher training strategies may solve part of the problem if they foster the formation of teacher self-support networks amongst neighboring schools, for example grouping teachers in teacher training workshops.

2.2.4 Culture

Rural areas have more profound links with their surrounding community than urban schools. Rural communities normally have less technological resources and more restricted information sources, conditions that are normally perceived as negative by people from more urban education areas who feel social or professional isolation in rural settings. Therefore it is important to realize that ICT can have an impact on the community as well.

The Enlaces experience shows that parents will normally regard the introduction of computers and Internet in their schools as a positive modernization effort and will stimulate their children to take advantage of the new educational resources. Students who may never hope to have computers at home will be more motivated to attend schools, looking forward to have a chance to explore and "play" with new machines. In most cases, teachers will also have a very positive reaction, perceiving the new opportunities provided by the ICT as a professional upgrade that makes their conditions closer to those of their urban colleagues.

Rural teachers are used to working under severe conditions with very scarce resources. Out of necessity they are used to solving problems in the schools in creative ways. This positive attitude can be a very powerful change force for innovation in a rural learning environment (Fullan 2000; Hargreaves 1994). Teacher training initiatives take this attitude into consideration when it comes to the choice of software, content, as well as learning practices appropriate and relevant for this reality.

It is also a reality that some communities that have a strong cultural identity (i.e., ethnic groups) sometimes feel, at least initially, that technology should be resisted as a cultural "invasion" from the dominant groups. This is a potential risk that has to be recognised and dealt with carefully but it is also the case that the groups may come to value technology as a powerful means to better represent and preserve their own cultural identity.

3. TEACHER TRAINING PROGRAM

The Enlaces teacher training strategy is designed to address the special conditions of rural schools. Training is regarded as a process of cultural appropriation because the way technology is used in rural schools is distant from teachers' current cultural practices. The integration of technology is a progressive process, requiring initial external support to help the teacher to actually participate in practices that integrate technology for pedagogical aims. This is seen as a "scaffolding" process in which an external "facilitator" works with the teacher within her/his "zone of proximal development" (Crook 1991; Ertmer 2001; Vygotsky 1978).

As an example of the training program, the goals of the teachers' first year of training are as follows (Enlaces 2001):

- Identify and use ICT resources that could support curricular activities inside the classroom — usually a word processor, a spreadsheet, painting software and various educational software packages related to early literacy and arithmetic. The software should meet the teachers' preferences and their students' needs. Teachers should understand how to organize the resources for classroom uses and for maximum student participation.
- Select, adapt, design and perform from three to five educational activities where students may use ICT resources. Teachers will have a set of sample activities to start with but should later be capable of designing their own. Collaborative work is strongly promoted as a learning strategy and is also used during the training itself, i.e., with groups of teachers.

The core of the teacher training program lasts for three years and is organized around the following three strands:

1. Basic ICT Skills Workshops: During the first two years teachers from one or two microcenters meet together and attend four workshops (nine days in total). The workshops are designed for teachers to achieve the basic skills required to use the equipment, basic software (Office-style packages) and explore new educational software that they might receive in the future.
2. In-classroom sessions where, during the three years of core training, the facilitator goes to each classroom during monthly visits to schools. In each visit s/he and the teacher work together with students in the implementation of pedagogical activities supported by ICT.
3. Microcenter sessions when, after each visit to the school, the facilitator and all the teachers from the microcenter meet together in a regular microcenter meeting. In the meetings they reflect and design together in relation to the integration of ICT in their teaching.

During the initial three years of teacher training, schools also receive regular technical support visits. Technicians working for the universities solve basic configuration problems, help teachers diagnose hardware problems and support them with the warranty procedures as well as train them in basic technical procedures such as virus disinfecting, file backup, and other management functions. After the three year period, all schools will receive permanent basic support intended to keep the technological infrastructure working and keep a pedagogical link with university consultants.

Given the relative isolation of rural teachers, trainers must work to develop the highest possible levels of teachers' autonomy. A set of self-training materials are part of the learning toolkits. If e-mail is available, teachers belonging to a microcenter are strongly encouraged to communicate and construct a community of apprenticeship. To promote that attitude, during the monthly meeting with the trainers, teachers are encouraged to share their experiences, problems and solutions. Finally, between meetings, each teacher will have specific work to accomplish with students, and will have to present and discuss its outcome with the rest of the teachers in the next meeting.

The quality of teacher trainers is essential to the initiative. The trainers belong to a group of specially selected teachers who must have experience working with ICT in their own schools for at least one year and their background should also include previous experience as primary teachers, if possible experience in rural education. Each trainer works with an average of 15 rural schools and, due to his/her own permanent training needs, normally works full time as a teacher trainer in close relation with one of the universities related to Enlaces.

Trainers must participate in collaborative training sessions for themselves during their first year as trainers. Besides developing strong ICT skills and experience in their use, part of their training includes an understanding of the educational reform and of the Chilean rural socio-economic reality. They must also understand the different approaches to ICT in education, the various motivational skills that might work with teachers and develop the technical skills needed to keep the ICT infrastructure in a school up and running. If necessary, trainers must also acquire an understanding of the indigenous culture and learning traditions.

3.1 Community Involvement

Parents and other members of the community surrounding the school are invited to participate in ICT-related activities in the school. The activities are designed by the teachers who, with the help of the students, teach adults the different uses of ICT. E-mail is specially appreciated but also Internet browsing so the community can read the news and learn about prices at the urban main shops.

The integration of parents has various positive side-effects for the school. First, by learning how to use computers, parents appreciate their possibilities and are more willing to support the school with time and small amounts of money for computer supplies, software or hardware purchases, upgrades and repairs. Second, by having a closer relationship with the school, parents become more interested and supportive of the school in general and therefore of their children's learning advances. Finally, the parents can use technology to expand their information sources and enhance their decision-making processes. Opening the parents to the rural schools that participate in Enlaces is regarded as a step forward toward bridging the digital divide.

4. CONCLUSIONS

Rural schools' special conditions (infrastructure, location, size, and local culture) pose a number of requirements and offer special opportunities for an educational ICT strategy. Teacher training should include a more thorough understanding of hardware and software issues to cope with maintenance and configuration problems that are normally dealt with by technicians in urban schools; teachers in small isolated schools with scarce resources normally have a positive attitude towards ICT for their own professional development. If Internet is available, it can be used as an important source of general news, educational tools and resources, and as a means of keeping in contact with other teachers.

Learning may be significantly enhanced when different grades share the same room by working collaboratively with ICT resources. If Internet access is available, students participate in world-wide projects such as I*Earn and WorldLinks, and will find content that is relevant for their personal interests, such as music, arts and sports. If Internet is not available, phone lines may allow for e-mail connections. Otherwise, CD-based content simulating a restricted Internet environment is used.

REFERENCES

Burniske, R.W. and Monke, L. (2001) *Breaking Down the Digital Walls.* Albany: State University of New York Press.

Campos, M., Cerda, C., Villarroel, J. and Rivera, R. (1998) Los proyectos colaborativos interescolares en la red Enlaces. *Revista Frontera, Edición Especial 17* Universidad de La Frontera, Temuco.

Crook, C. (1991) Computers in the zone of proximal development: implications for evaluation. *Computers in Education* 17 1 81-91.

Crook, C. (1994) *Computers and the Collaborative Experience of Learning*. London: Routledge.

Enlaces, C.Z.S.-A.d. (2001) *Uso progresivo de la informática en el aula multigrado*. Centro Zonal Sur-Austral, Instituto de Informática Educativa. Universidad de La Frontera, Temuco.

Ertmer, P.A. (2001) Responsive Instructional Design: Scaffolding the adoption and change process. *Educational Technology* 41 6 33-38.

Fullan, M. (2000) *Changing Forces*. London: Falmer Press.

Githiora-Updike, W. (2000) The global schoolhouse. In D. T. Gordon (ed.) *The Digital Classroom*. Cambridge, MA: Harvard Education Letter.

Hargreaves, A. (1994) *Changing Teachers, Changing Times*. London: Cassell.

Hepp, P. (1999) Enlaces: Todo un mundo para los niños y jóvenes de Chile. In C. Cox (ed.) *La Reforma Educacional Chilena*. Santiago, Chile: Editorial Popular 289-303.

Hepp, P., Alvarez, M.I., Hinostroza, E. and Laval, E. (1993) La Plaza: A software design for an educational network. In the *Proceedings of the Ed-Media '93 World Conference on Educational Multimedia an Hypermedia*. Orlando Florida, EEUU.

I*Earn. International Education and Resource Network. <http://www.iearn.org/>.

San Miguel, J. (1999) Programa de Educación Básica Rural. In J.E. García-Huidobro (ed.) *La Reforma Educacional Chilena*. Madrid: Editorial Popular.

Think.com. Oracle Corporation. <http://d1.think.com/>.

Trucano, M. and Hawkins, R. (2002) Getting a school on-line in a developing country: Common mistakes, technology options and costs. *TechKnowLogia* (January-March 2002) 54-58.

Vygotsky, L.S. (1978) *Mind in Society*. Cambridge, MA: Harvard University Press.

Wenger, E. (1998) *Communities of Practice:Learning, Meaning, and Identity*. Cambridge: Cambridge University Press.

Worldlinks. Enlaces mundiales para el desarrollo. Instituto del Banco Mundial. <http://www.worldbank.org/worldlinks/spanish/>.

BIOGRAPHIES

Pedro Hepp received his degree in engineering from the Pontificia Universidad Católica de Chile (1976) and has a Ph.D. in Computer Science from Edinburgh University (1983). He is head of "Enlaces" (1990–2001) and of the "Community Networks" project (2000-2002). A director of Instituto de Informática Educativa, Universidad de La Frontera, Chile (1996-2001) and a full professor at that university, he was an Associate Professor at the Computer Science Department, Pontificia Universidad Católica de Chile (1976-1992) and is now principal researcher of several FONDECYT (Conicyt, Chilean research funding agency) projects on software engineering, multimedia, expert systems and education.

Ernesto Laval is an engineer and has a M.Sc. degree from the Pontificia Universidad Católica de Chile. He is completing his Ph.D. at Bristol

University and presently works at the Instituto de Informática Educativa from Universidad de La Frontera in Temuco, Chile. Since 1991 he has been involved in the design and implementation of "Enlaces". In 1999 he was appointed as the coordinator of the rural chapter of Enlaces, and he is currently working with the Ministry of Education in the design of the Chilean strategy for literacy and numeracy in primary education.

National plans and local challenges

Preparing for lifelong learning in a digital society

Sindre Røsvik
Giske kommune, N-6050 Valderøy Norway; sindre@mimer.no

Abstract: This paper presents a case study of a Norwegian primary school as an example of the approach used to introduce Information and Communication Technology (ICT) policy in Norway. After an overview of Norwegian school system and national goals for ICT in education, the paper describes the challenges teachers and schools face when implementing curricula designed to fulfill different national expectations, ranging from specific skills and pieces of knowledge to more general goals such as preparing students for the future society. National curriculum guidelines describe what should be taught and what skills should be mastered but local schools and teachers must do the actual implementation. The most important actor in the Norwegian classroom is the student while the teacher creates stimulating learning environments. Learning to learn and lifelong learning are considered the main tasks of schools. This paper presents a programme of a lower primary school (6 to 10 year-olds) which has taken up the challenge of focusing on learning to learn, including use of ICT. Skjong barneskule, where learning to learn and learning how to use ICT is combined with development of a richer learning environment and learning specific knowledge, exemplifies the Norwegian programme.

Key words: elementary education, conditions for learning, organising for learning, collaboration

1. INTRODUCTION

1.1 Education in Norway

During the last decades the Norwegian educational system has undergone a series of reforms. Education and the development of skills have a high political priority in achieving highest academic standards. The goals include learning for the largest possible proportion of the population. It is hoped that the plans will improve the quality of life for the individual as well as increase productivity. Equal opportunities and the right to education for all have the highest priority in our unified educational system (Education in Norway 1997).

In 2001 a revised version of eNorway was introduced to plan for ICT use throughout the country. The overall aim was to promote a "green knowledge" economy equivalent to the eEurope programme but with extra, specific-to-Norway goals since Norway was ranked as the world's second-best information economy in February 2001. It is no wonder that education should emphasise learning opportunities that include ICT use for every Norwegian. The innovative Project for Innovation, Learning and Organisational development and Technology (PILOT), part of the initiative, represents a major effort to initiate and support educational changes and says that holistic approaches are necessary to achieve substantial and sustainable changes.

Earlier, curriculum guidelines (L97) were introduced and compulsory schooling was extended from nine to ten years by lowering the school starting age to six year-olds so compulsory education is now organised in three main stages: Primary school (preschool to grade four); middle school (grades five to seven); and lower secondary (grades eight to ten).

"Inclusion" is the key concept and means that everybody, regardless of background or physical abilities, should be included and belong to an ordinary school and class.

1.2 ICT in primary education

The curriculum guidelines for primary and secondary education for the 13 years of schooling emphasise holistic human perspectives and call for increasing knowledge learning as well as learning basic skills. Norwegian educators believe plans should take into account challenges not yet known so students need to be prepared to tackle ongoing developments and changes. Learning to learn and the ability to adapt to new situations are seen as basic skills.

In the digital society competencies such as use of digital media and computers are required. Computers and electronic learning materials are considered useful in cross-curricular areas of knowledge and it is emphasised that students should develop knowledge, insight and attitudes about the development of the Information Society and Information Technology. The Norwegian position is that students ought to develop the ability to use electronic tools and media critically and constructively. They should also be able to use ICT as practical tools for subject learning, for themes and for projects. ICT offers the possibility of using national and international databases, and both girls and boys should be stimulated to use ICT to prevent development of social or gender differences (L97). Norwegian curriculum guidelines also emphasise that students shall be encouraged to be active, initiating and independent:

> ICT is to be used in education in order to contribute to better organisation, greater skills and pedagogical competence within an education system that develops and exploits ICT as a subject. The potential of ICT is to be exploited within teaching and learning so that the skills requirements of the individual and the society as a whole can be met (L97).

Norwegian ICT goals should also prepare students for new forms of cooperation, work, learning and assessment, and provide individuals who have learning difficulties with opportunities to improve the quality of their lives and join a communal work force.

Action plans for 2002 (Utdannings- og forskningsdepartmentet 2002) emphasise that ICT in education aims at improving the learning environment. Successful implementation identifies implementation barriers and aims at developing a national learning grid with new forms of examination and assessment. The development of electronic learning materials along with support for the use of ICT in different subjects and cross-curricular work is also a priority.

Development of teacher competencies is given a high priority with substantial resources allocated. Infrastructure improvement and maintenance, as well as cooperation between different levels of the education system are important as are access to equipment and access to broadband.

2. GISKE KOMMUNE: A COMMUNITY BLENDING OLD AND NEW

Giske kommune is an island community consisting of four islands connected by bridges and sub-sea tunnels. The population of the islands and the district is growing. The airport of the region is located at Vigra, one of the islands, and has good connections to international flights via Oslo. The district's business is international. Over the last 100 years the region has been exporting fish to Europe and, over the last decades, to Brazil, the USA and Asia. Trading of timber has long been important since historically the Vikings were not only warriors but also peaceful traders. Now shipbuilding design and equipment are exported worldwide. In some niches district industries have links and production sites with companies around the world. So the people of the Giske kommune have always been open-minded and prepared to go abroad to acquire new competencies to bring back home. The kommune hopes to continue the tradition of sending its sons and daughters abroad but seeing them return to continue the maintenance of community traditions. It may be the same open-mindedness to change that generates acceptance of ICT as a tool for the future of Giske's young and old.

The Internet is considered a useful resource for all levels of teaching and learning. It should be noted that we deliberately do not use any kind of filtering technology, even for the youngest children. However teachers do monitor closely Internet use. Ethical perspectives and critical attitudes are taught from an early age. Only one complaint has surfaced concerning students visiting improper sites and this was dealt with in a way that taught the student the values of the community.

Schools in our municipality have participated in different national ICT projects since 1984. It is unusual for such a small community to participate in several different national projects. But Skjong barneskule, a primary school stage 1-4 (ages 6-11 years) in the kommune, has never been considered an outstanding school although they work in a systematic way with ICT. As municipal director, I must ensure that the school, along with other schools on the islands, provide equal opportunities, focus on relevant outcomes and participate in the use of national ICT resources.

2.1 Teaching and learning with ICT: Skjong barneskule for 6 to 10 year-olds

Skjong barneskule has chosen to introduce and use ICT with children in the same way they work with other subjects and themes. Teachers lecture to children, working quite traditionally, but for several lessons a week more and more students work on their own by following work-plans called "study lessons". So changes in methods and organising are taking place. During the coming year each student will make his/her own plan of study, concretising the aims of the national curriculum linked to their own interests and abilities. The activities will include: "This is me ..." (self presentation) and continue with "I am good at ... , I like ... , and I can ..." as well as "My goals, actions to achieve the first step are ..." and culminating with "Evaluation, what were the results?" Of course they work with their teachers along the way but they also become aware of their own roles and responsibilities.

Children are also expected to take charge of their own learning by searching and constructing their own knowledge, and are trained in this learning approach. It is considered important to share ideas and competencies contributing to building a better society — "designing and building our common future" (UNESCO 1996). Taking charge of your local community is considered an important value. The concept of learning throughout life emerges as one of the keys to the 21st century (UNESCO 1996).

Skjong has also integrated learning into the community by inviting grandparents to learn ICT from the children. The children demonstrate the Internet and explain how to use it for information and communication purposes.

So how do the children learn to use computers, and what kind of access do they have? The school has 15 computers for 80 students and the computer lab is equipped with nine computers. There is also one computer per classroom and two special needs students have their own computers. The computer lab is a group room situated between the classroom of the third and fourth graders with access directly from both classrooms. As part of their programme students are allowed to go to the computers, and normally they organise queuing and use of computers between themselves but sometimes teachers have to mediate and guide the children for a more purposeful use and organisation.

Learning how to take responsibility for their own learning allows children to decide what methods and material they will use, and when to go to the computer lab to fulfil tasks to be solved or to play with the computers to develop and maintain their computer skills. As prescribed in the curriculum, students should learn certain abilities at each class level. The school has developed a nine-stage computer certificate programme where those abilities are included. Instead of the teacher introducing each theme or certificate, the students teach each other. In this way several aims of the curriculum are fulfilled. Normally, third or four graders teach the younger ones. The goals of the certificates are listed below. The certificates are related to specific goals and progress according to the curriculum, but children may follow a faster progression when they are interested in doing so as shown by a sample in Table 1.

2.1.1 Certificate achievement

The certificates issued to children are supposed to be achieved at the following levels:

- Computer certificate 1: Put together a jigsaw puzzles: first grade autumn;
- Computer certificate 2: Use educational software: first grade spring;
- Computer certificate 3: Use MSWord and enter letters of the alphabet: second grade autumn;

- Computer certificate 4: Use MSWord and write words and sentences: second grade spring;
- Computer certificate 5: Go to the homepage of school: third grade autumn;
- Computer certificate 6: Save text in a file on the hard disk and print: third grade autumn;
- Computer certificate 7: Save text to a diskette and print: third grade spring;
- Computer certificate 8: Go to the Internet, search for themes and print: fourth grade autumn;
- Computer certificate 9: Use MSExcel: fourth grade spring.

Table 1. Computer Certificate 1 issued when a student acquires the skills

Computer Certificate 1	
Name of student	
I am able to:	Turn on the computer
	Write my password
	Find and put together the puzzle
	Terminate and turn off the computer
Signed by the teacher _______	

When students claim that they have mastered skills, they approach their teachers to be tested and, if they are able to prove their abilities, the teacher gives them the certificate which they then bring to the computer lab. They are only supposed to work with programmes and tasks they are certified to use. In cases of misuse the teacher may withdraw their right to work on their own with computers. For example, if they are just surfing purposelessly on the Internet or searching sites not approved, their right to use the computer may be terminated. Even young students are able to help each other by explaining how to learn and use ICT. A child with Downs syndrome received certificate 1 and 2 and that made him very happy.

The programme is presented at the school's homepage <http://www.skjong.gs.mr.no/> where other activities and projects are also presented. Typically, the children use many pictures to document activities. The idea of using certificates may seem to be a gimmick but it works. After they master the computer they also use other programs such as Word Art.

The children have used this program to make a "reading diploma" to be handed out to those who have read a certain amount of time (100, 250, 500, 1 000 minutes). This has become a very popular way of increasing reading and reading ability. Students get a clear understanding of what is to be learned and what to explain their fellow students. The teachers are amazed to observe how well-behaved, self-confident and able the students are at instructing grown-ups such as their grandparents to find their way on the Internet.

ICT for the children is just another source of information. Sometimes they prefer using ordinary books but working on a project about universe with the Internet was found to be a unique way to learn and some were able to find their way by using sites written in English. But since they will not be fluent in English for some years to come Norwegian sites are preferred by the children. The headmaster of Skjong reports that when the children gain certificate 5, the homepage of Skjong barneskule is used from the homes more. Some families have even chosen the homepage of Skjong barneskule as their Internet starting page, meaning they closely follow the activities of the school.

The most important learning, however, is that the children learn to learn and to help others learn. The programme applied at Skjong barneskule supports children to progressively find the most effective ways of learning and the best ways to act responsibly, especially in situations where they are working together with others. Observing the children at work confirms that: (1) they show greater social reciprocity adapting to each other and the environment; (2) they are taking greater personal responsibility for their own actions and consequences of these for others; (3) they act in more comprehensive and culturally appropriate ways; and (4) they work with enhanced motivation, allowing for a greater variation of alternative actions (Appelberg and Eriksson 2001).

The children develop social and emotional competencies along with acquiring subject knowledge and skills. The computer turns out to be a social tool enhancing abilities to work together. Children wait for turns and help each other. If children are guided or instructed too strictly by teachers negative consequences may be the result and the usefulness of computers reduced.

During the last three years parents and politicians have been included in quality assurance inspections. The educational advisor plans the inspections with the educational director. The actual inspection takes only one day but the schools prepare by doing an internal evaluation with a defined focus. The politicians and parents say that they are very impressed with what they see and experience. They are satisfied that the children are content, open-minded and self-confident. More than one grown up has said that they "envy" their children being students in such a school. The organising of ICT is also praised, not least because it provides equal access to children regardless of their access at home. Some parents also say that they were not aware of the potential of ICT for supporting children's learning of basic skills and other subjects.

3. CONCLUSION

The results at Skjong barneskule show that teacher instruction is reduced, allowing children to support each other in playing and learning situations. Children are encouraged to take responsibility for their own learning and their own social environment, while the teacher tends to be more a facilitator and guide. The computer is not the primary focus, but rather the focus is on interaction between computer and children as well as the social learning. Cooperation is given focus, not only individual learning.

On the whole, teachers report that children are learning to learn using different sources and methods in a meaningful and effective way. Working with textbooks, traditional workbooks, singing, playing and making real models of paper or other materials are more commonly used than the Internet or other ICT-based tools. Both teachers and children are comfortable with the situation as it is. Use of ICT is still limited by access to computers and the availability of suitable software.

REFERENCES

Appelberg, L. and Eriksson, M. (2001) *Barn erobrer datamaskinen – en utfordring for de voksne* (Children conquer the computer – a challenge to the grown ups). Oslo: Kommuneforlaget AS.

Kirke-, utdannings- og forskningsdepartementet (2000) *Handlingsplan – IKT i norsk utdanning - Plan for 2000 - 2003.* (Ministry of Education, Research and Church Affairs: Action plan - ICT in Norwegian Education - Plan for 2000 - 2003) Oslo: Kirke-, utdannings- og forskningsdepartementet.

Kirke-, utdannings- og forskningsdepartementet (1997) *Education in Norway* (Ministry of Education, Research and Church Affairs). Oslo: Kirke-, utdannings- og forsknings-departementet.

Kirke-, utdannings- og forskningsdepartementet. (1996) *Læreplanverket for den 10-årige grunnskolen* (Curriculum Guidelines for the 10-Year Compulsory School). Oslo: Kirke-, utdannings- og forskningsdepartementet.

UNESCO. (1996) *Learning: The Treasure Within.* Report to UNESCO of the International Commission on Education for the Twenty-first Century. Paris: UNESCO.

BIOGRAPHY

Sindre Røsvik is the municipal director of the Giske municipality where Skjong barneskule is situated. He is the founding chairman of the Norwegian Educational Computer Society, a longstanding member of IFIP's Working Group 3.5 (Informatics in Elementary Education) and presently serves as its chairman.

Learning online

E-learning and the domestic market in the UK

Margaret Scanlon and David Buckingham
Institute of Education, University of London, 20 Bedford Way, London WC1H OAL; m.scanlon@ioe.ac.uk; d.buckingham@ioe.ac.uk

Abstract: Over the past decade the Internet has become a vital educational resource. In this paper we look at the growing e-learning industry, focusing on the conflict of interests which has emerged between the public and private sectors. We also look at the impact of new media on the demand for more traditional media.

Key words: sites of learning, policy

1. INTRODUCTION

In the past decade, the home has become an increasingly important educational site. The British government's evangelistic emphasis on education now extends well beyond its efforts to raise "standards" in schools. Funding is currently available for a whole range of new initiatives that seek to extend the reach of schooling into children's leisure time. The steady extension of national testing has created an atmosphere of growing competition, not only between schools but also among parents and children. Education, it would seem, is the work of childhood, and it cannot be allowed to stop once children walk out of the classroom door.

Commercial companies have not been slow to grasp those opportunities. Parents are under increasing pressure to "invest" in their children's education by providing additional resources at home, most computer manufacturers claiming they can "help" your child to get ahead in the educational race (Nixon 1998; Buckingham, Scanlon and Sefton-Green 2001). Currently sales of educational materials designed for domestic use, for example, in the form of study guides and early learning materials, are booming. Private home tutoring is becoming more common and there has been a marked increase in the commercial provision of supplementary classes, not just in "extras" such as the arts but also in "basics" such as maths and literacy. The marketing of such goods and services often seeks to appeal to parents' "better nature" — their sense of what they *should* be doing in order to qualify as Good Parents.

On one level, commercial involvement in out-of-school learning is nothing new. There is a long history of parents providing educational resources at home. Luke (1989) and others have pointed out that the modern "invention" of childhood was accompanied by a whole range of pedagogic initiatives aimed at parents and children, including primers, advice manuals and instructional books and playthings. However the nature and scale of the operation have significantly changed in recent years. Technological developments, government policy and market forces have combined to bring about those changes.

The Internet shows the greatest potential for extending learning into the home. The number of homes with computers and Internet access has increased steadily over the last few years, thus increasing the potential for electronic learning. In this paper, which is drawn from an ongoing research project, we consider the current state of the e-learning industry, the growing market for educational web sites and the impact on the market for more traditional media. Our work is based on an analysis of the educational publishing industry, drawing on the trade press, market research reports and interviews with publishers and software/web site producers.

2. THE INTERNET AND HOME LEARNING

New media play an increasingly important role in education, both at home and in schools. Enthusiasts argue that computers have the potential to engage and motivate pupils in ways that conventional classroom teaching does not. Children are assumed to have a natural aptitude and enthusiasm for computers (whereas adults do not); and computers are seen to make learning automatically more interesting and exciting. In one of the more effusive treatises on this subject, Seymour Papert (1996) describes the "passionate love affair" between children and computers. On a more pragmatic level, familiarity with computers is now seen as important for the future of the "e-economy". Partly for those reasons, the Department for Education and Science (DfES) is committed to connecting all schools to the Internet and e-mail by the end of 2002. The Institute for Public Policy Research has recommended that they go further and ensure universal Internet access for everyone from the home (Tambini 2000).

One key aspect of new media is their potential to extend the reach of schooling beyond the classroom. Computers are helping to break down some of the traditional barriers in terms of age and location: Education is no longer seen merely as something that takes place in a school/college/university between the ages of 5 and 21 (or beyond). Many commentators are predicting that in the future the home will become a more important site for education because children will be accessing information and classes via the Internet (Loveless and Ellis 2001). Michael Hargreaves, Chief Executive of the Qualifications and Curriculum Authority (QCA), predicted that "quite soon we shall see sixth formers spending up to half their time out of school, undertaking learning at home and in other places" (Buckingham and McFarlane 2001).

2.1 Concerns about e-learning

Despite the optimism and utopian rhetoric that often surrounds discussions about new media and education, a number of concerns have also been raised. The so-called digital divide between those who have access to home computers and those who do not has been well documented (BECTa 2001).

Even in cases where children do have access to a computer, such access does not automatically mean that it will be used for educational purposes. Differential access to the Internet at home may also be influenced by parental attitudes towards the Internet and by the cultural resources that a family can bring to bear (Furlong, et al. 2000). Another important use is whether ICT is capable of making any real difference to education and whether there has been a sufficient return on the huge investment made. A report published by the US-based Alliance for Childhood argues that there is no clear evidence that primary school children have made any gains as a result of technology use (Coughlan 2001). The report also asks what advances might have been achieved if similar amounts of money had been pumped into smaller class sizes, more teachers, more books or better school buildings. Despite the concerns, the number of homes with computers and Internet access continues to rise steadily. Computers have been heavily marketed as an educational resource and lack of access to the Internet at home is now seen as a serious disadvantage in educational terms (Nixon 1998).

3. OLD AND NEW MEDIA

One indicator of the growing importance of the Internet in home education is the effect that it has had on the market for print media and software. Competition from the Internet has led to a decline in demand for glossy reference books, especially encyclopaedias and atlases. Problems for publishers in that sector started several years ago when CD-ROMs were first developed and computer companies decided to include reference packages such as Encarta with their computers. Now encyclopaedias are available free on the Internet and there are hundreds of sites linked to museums, libraries, art galleries, etc. in direct competition with the reference book market.

The Internet also has a number of advantages over print in terms of providing more powerful search tools and hyperlinks with related sites. It invariably influences what publishers decide to produce and how they produce it. Some are reluctant to publish encyclopaedias and atlases since those can be updated on the Internet. Publishers are also wary of subjects such as geography, where content can be broken down into "sound bites" suitable for web sites. They try not to replicate information that is already on the Internet or look for different ways of approaching a subject. It is also evident that digital media are influencing the visual style of print texts and the ways in which they structure the reader's access to information. For example, a representative of one of the main reference publishers in the UK told us they were planning to use more computer graphics in their books because children are so familiar with those types of images. The idea is to make the transition from computer screens to books seem less great.

The market for CD-ROMs has also been affected. According to representatives of the main software producers, the market has started to slow down over the last few years, largely due to competition from the Internet. In the UK, concerns have even been raised about the future of school broadcasting. According to Robin Moss, former head of educational broadcasting at the Independent Television Commission, the BBC's school broadcasting service is being under-funded and undermined in the drive to create electronic learning resources (Brown 2002), a claim which the BBC vehemently denies (Stevenson 2002).

Despite competition from the Internet, reference publishers and software companies are not facing imminent ruin. Books still have many advantages over digital media. They are portable, easily accessible and, according to publishers, have greater authority because they have been through an editorial process. Furthermore, some parents are wary about letting their children use the Internet or may not have access to the Internet for economic reasons, although, by the same token, those parents may also be unable to afford books or software. Nevertheless, the advantages of CD-ROMs as compared to the Internet are increasingly difficult to identify.

The most obvious strategy for publishers and software companies is to find ways of using the Internet to their own advantage. Some are developing their own sites or becoming content providers for others, effectively using the Internet as another means of distributing content. Others are building connections between books or CD-ROMs and dedicated web sites to which purchasers will have restricted access. Overall, publishers seem to be rethinking their role and re-inventing themselves as information providers across different media. This is undoubtedly a testing time for publishers as they enter the unpredictable e-learning market.

4. THE E-LEARNING INDUSTRY

The e-learning industry is only just beginning to take shape, with many different players jostling for position in a very competitive market. A few of the companies involved have a public service obligation to offer educational content, the BBC and Channel 4 for example. Others are commercial companies, often with a stake in other media and/or education, for example the Times Educational Supplement (TES) and The Guardian. Software companies are especially interested in the possibilities of the Internet because of the decline in the CD-ROM market. Companies such as Europress and The Learning Company are now planning to develop their own web sites or become content providers for others. Apart from those commercial providers, non-profit organisations, schools and individuals are also creating educational web sites.

Although, in theory, anyone with access to the Internet can create a web site, there can be little doubt that established content providers in other media are particularly well favoured. Concerns about quality control on the Internet mean that companies with an established brand in other areas of the media or education, the BBC for example, have a distinct advantage if they develop web sites. Multimedia conglomerates such as Pearson or Vivendi are also in an ideal position to create educational sites because they already have access to content through their ownership of publishing and software companies. When the educational web site <education.com> was created in 2001, it was able to draw on a number of properties owned by its parent company, Vivendi. Thus, according to information on the web site, <education.com> offers rich and varied content from major print publishers: Chambers-Harrap, Kingfisher, Larousse, Retz; and multimedia publishers: Coktel and its famous characters Adi and Adiboo, Knowledge Adventure and its Jump Ahead and Blaster Rangers. Similarly, Pearson is able to use content from its publishing subsidiaries Penguin and Dorling Kindersley in its online education material. In this respect, technological changes reinforce the tendency of changing patterns of ownership to create a more centralised industry. There has been a convergence of media, with companies like Granada having a stake in publishing, TV, software and, now, e-learning.

But e-learning and e-publishing are still in the developmental stage and one of the main issues facing commercial companies is how to make a return on their investment. The basic means of funding (or generating profit) is still uncertain. Subscriptions and advertising are two of the leading possibilities. Spark Learning, for example, has developed an elaborate system for generating income based on advertising, subscription fees from parents and schools, and sponsorship from London Electricity. In addition, the site has links to WH Smith and other retailers. There are also examples of companies developing sites which effectively have to be used in conjunction with other media, either print or digital. So, for example, Pearson have launched a study guides package comprising online testing and resources which can be accessed only by students who have purchased the book. Meanwhile, software producers are developing CD-ROMs that allow users to download additional content from the Internet.

While selling advertising space is common practice, some companies have taken a step further by setting up education web sites which essentially promote their own products or services. The Cadbury site is one example of how education, entertainment and advertising have been combined. Launched in 2000, the Cadbury Learning Zone is a free site aimed at the home and school, and purports to make learning "fun". There are three subject areas — maths, history and the environment — and separate information sections for parents and teachers. It is to be expected that the Cadbury brand name would be featured prominently, but most of the learning activities are based on a chocolate theme or linked to Cadbury. The maths section, for example, features "Mr. Cadbury's Chocolate Factory" and the characters are all named after chocolate products ("Buttons", "Fudge", "Curly Wurly" and "Chomp").

The history section focuses on the history of Cadbury. Only the environment part of the site does not focus specifically on chocolate and Cadbury, but the characters ("Yowies") feature in Cadbury products. The rationale behind setting learning activities in a "chocolate factory" is explained as follows: "Using as a focus the realistic context of maths in chocolate making, children will be able to gain an appreciation of the value of maths in a real working situation." Elsewhere the producers state that the Learning Zone is part of Cadbury's wider commitment to education, both within "our own communities" and at a national level. A more cynical view might be that the site provides a good deal of covert advertising for Cadbury.

Interestingly, the Cadbury Learning Zone is a National Grid for Learning-approved site and is affiliated with Gridclub, the Bafta-winning DfES/Channel 4 site. In that context it is not surprising that the NGfL portal has in the past been criticised for its lack of substantive content: Comparisons have been made between the site and New Labour's other flagship project, the ill-fated Millennium Dome.

Apart from the business models outlined above, another important source of funding is through the government. Government policy in the last five years has done much to create the potential for an e-learning industry. As part of the NGfL initiative it has spent approximately £1bn equipping schools with computers, training teachers and developing the NGfL portal. Commercial companies played an important part in the rollout of the NGfL and they clearly intend to be involved in the development of digital content for homes and schools. However, the emerging industry has from the start been characterised by a certain amount of tension between public and private sectors, which reflects broader developments in the "marketisation" of education (Gewirtz, Ball and Bowe 1995). The current debate over plans to create a digital curriculum brought these tensions to the forefront. As the government's plans for the provision of digital content became more ambitious they also became more contentious as commercial companies saw them as encroaching on their territory.

5. THE DIGITAL CURRICULUM

By 2001 the NGfL was one of the largest educational portals in Europe but, as noted above, it lacked substantial content. For commercial providers, this represented an enormous opportunity. Clearly the government was going to continue to play a significant role, but there were differences of opinion over what that role should be.

Much of the debate about government involvement has centred around the issue of whether it should foster a supply- or demand-led market for e-learning. In the supply-led (or "top-down") model, the government would commission companies to produce content that would be free to users. Alternatively, it could authorise a state-subsidised organisation (in this case the BBC) to produce content. The demand-led model would involve funding being made available directly to users so that they could select and pay for the sites they want, which in turn would stimulate content production. The essence of this view is that the market will inevitably provide. Not surprisingly, commercial companies generally prefer the latter option, whilst the BBC has campaigned persistently for the former. The fundamental opposition has been at the heart of an ongoing debate about the development of digital content for schools and homes.

Some of the DfES's early initiatives have been generally well received. GridClub is a free online service provided by Channel 4 in the UK in partnership with Intuitive Media and Oracle, and funded by £6 million from the DfES. Designed to be used by children at home or at school, GridClub received good reviews in the press and has won a number of awards, though take-up has not been as high as expected. The DfES also funded a £5 million pilot project to develop courses in maths, Latin and Japanese at Key Stage 3. Content was developed by Granada Learning, the BBC and RM, and press reports suggest that the pilots were a success (Cole 2002). However, the initiatives were soon to be overshadowed by the controversy surrounding the BBC's plans for a digital curriculum.

In 2000 the BBC issued a consultation document outlining proposals to provide national curriculum learning materials free to users over the Internet and through digital TV. The project was to be funded through the license fee and would target both the school and the home market. The BBC justified its plans in terms of its track record in providing learning materials and its public service obligation to support education. Not surprisingly, the plans met with opposition from the commercial sector. In their view, allowing a state-subsidised body to spend up to £150m of license fees on developing digital content was tantamount to creating a public monopoly. Commercial companies argued that the planned digital curriculum was anti-competitive and would effectively exclude them from the growing digital education market. Like previous episodes in the development of the NGfL, the industry's views were often couched in altruistic or utopian terms, concerning "choice for schools", "quality" and teachers becoming "the long-term losers" if the free market is not allowed to prevail (Selwyn 1999).

Commercial companies got the opportunity to voice their objections when the DfES set up its own consultation process in 2001. In addition, industry lobbied MPs and their views were published in the press and at public meetings. Questions were even asked in parliament. Interestingly, the views of schools, parents, and organisations such as the Parents Information Network were almost never reported in the press. Some of the most strident criticism of the BBC's plans came from Merlin John, editor of the TES Online, who regularly castigated the BBC's role, at one point describing the corporation as a "self-seeking organisation" which had "stumped up some cash in a back-room deal" (John 2001).

The suspicions and fears of the industry were further aroused in 2001 when the DfES awarded Granada and the BBC a £42 million contract to develop content for six General Certificate of Secondary Education (GCSE) subjects. Many companies object to such supply-led funding in principle, preferring direct funding to users, but the contract was also contentious because of the way in which it was awarded. The industry claimed that the terms of the original tender were changed: The tender appeared to discourage bids from non-TV companies, but it later transpired that most services were to be delivered online, not by television.

The debate rumbled on until the end of 2001 when a temporary compromise was reached. The government announced its plans for a "Curriculum Online" initiative whereby schools will receive £50 million in the form of "e-learning credits" to buy digital material. A content advisory panel will oversee the resources on offer, which will be available to homes as well as schools. At the same time the government announced that it would not be going ahead with the £42m award to Granada and the BBC. The secretary of state for education explained that the rapid development of technologies and the wider scope of Curriculum Online meant that the Department would not be proceeding with the initiative. However it appears that the BBC will go ahead with its plans for a digital curriculum, subject to approval by the Department for Culture, Media and Sport.

The Curriculum Online initiative seems to illustrate the increasing influence of the commercial sector in education and the conflicts of interest that can arise between public and private spheres. New Labour has from the start fostered commercial involvement in initiatives such as the NGfL but business interests will inevitably resist government interventions that appear to threaten their profitability. As Selwyn and Fitz (2001) have pointed out, handling the role of the private sector in what is very public policy is always going to be potentially problematic. In the debate over the provision of a digital curriculum the situation was made even more complicated by the involvement of the BBC. The dispute between the corporation and the commercial sector has not yet been resolved. In May 2000 a coalition of software firms were demanding a judicial review of the BBC's plans to spend £150m of licence money on developing the digital curriculum (Cassy 2002).

6. CONCLUSION

The rapid growth of educational web sites raises several questions that have a broader relevance to the contemporary study of education. The questions could be seen in terms of a set of changing relationships: Between the home and the school, between education and entertainment, and between the public and the private spheres. How the e-learning market "settles down" as it moves beyond the pioneering stage may well reveal a great deal about the future shape of educational markets and about the role the media are coming to play within them.

The home has become an increasingly important site for education, and initiatives such as the DfES's Curriculum Online and the BBC's digital curriculum have the potential to contribute to the trend. One of the clearly stated objectives of both initiatives is that they will provide content for schools *and* homes, and it is to be hoped that providers will distinguish between and cater for the needs of both groups. But there is a danger that the online education market will be dominated by provision for schools which is larger and more stable. As a result the material that is available to the home market may reflect a relatively narrow conception of learning. Already some of the main out-of-school learning sites are geared towards homework and revision, for example, Bitesize, revisewise, SOS Teacher and Homework High. The reality of electronic learning may be less exciting than the utopian scenarios described by Seymour Papert and others. Whilst revision and homework sites are no doubt useful, they are unlikely to engender "a passionate love affair" between children and computers.

However, it is too early to conclude that the domestic market for e-learning will be driven by exams and national curriculum objectives, partly because different companies work on the basis of different business models. Some non-fiction publishers, for example, are producing materials that are specifically *not* geared towards the curriculum of one country so that they can reach an international audience. Meanwhile museums, art galleries, libraries and voluntary organisations in the UK and elsewhere are starting to provide spaces on their web sites which are designed for children. It may be through these routes that children find alternative learning resources.

Of course, for those who do not have access to the Internet at home such options are not easily available. Indeed the public debate over the digital curriculum and who should provide it largely ignored the fact that many families do not have Internet access and that not all schools have the broadband connections necessary to take advantage of the new resources. Therefore, in the short-term at least, the initiatives are likely to perpetuate existing inequalities both between homes and also between schools.

REFERENCES

BECTa (2001) The "Digital Divide": A Discussion Paper. Coventry: BECTA.

Brown, M. (2002) Switched off. *The Guardian* 14 May.

Buckingham, D. and McFarlane, A. (2001) *A Digitally Driven Curriculum?* London: The Institute for Public Policy Research.

Buckingham, D., Scanlon, M. and Sefton-Green, J. (2001) Selling the digital dream: Marketing educational technology to teachers and parents. In A. Loveless and V. Ellis (eds.) *ICT, Pedagogy and the Curriculum: Subject to Change*. London: Routledge.
Cassy, J. (2002) Rivals threaten BBC with court for £150m online learning push. *The Guardian* 24th May.
Cole, G. (2002) The digital dilemma. *The Guardian* 8th January 2002.
Coughlan, S. (2001) Devil's advocate. *Times Educational Supplement: Online* 11th May.
Furlong, J., Furlong, R., Facer, K. and Sutherland, R. (2000) The National Grid for Learning: A curriculum without walls. *Cambridge Journal of Education* 30 1 91-110.
Gewirtz, S., Ball, S. and Bowe, R. (1995) *Markets, Choice and Equity in Education.* Buckingham: Open University Press.
John, M. (2001) Lifelong learning: Until 6 pm. *Times Educational Supplement Online* 9th November.
Loveless, A. and Ellis, V. (2001) *ICT, Pedagogy and the Curriculum: Subject to Change.* London: Routledge.
Luke, C. (1989) *Pedagogy, Printing and Protestantism: The Discourse on Childhood.* Albany, NY: SUNY Press.
Nixon, H. (1998) Fun and games are serious business. In J. Sefton-Green (ed.) *Digital Diversions: Youth Culture in the Age of Multimedia*. London: UCL Press.
Papert, S. (1996) *The Connected Family*. Atlanta: Longstreet Press.
Selwyn, N. (1999) "Gilding the Grid": The marketing of the National Grid for Learning. *British Journal of Sociology of Education* 20 1 59-72.
Selwyn, N. and Fitz, J. (2001) The National Grid for Learning: A case study of new labour education policy-making. *Journal of Education Policy* 16 2 127-147.
Stevenson, M. (2002) Auntie knows best. *The Guardian* 21 May.
Tambini, D. (2000) *Universal Internet Access*. London: London School of Economics and Political Science.

BIOGRAPHIES

Margaret Scanlon is a Research Officer in the Centre for the Study of Children, Youth and Media at the Institute of Education, University of London. The project on which she is currently working looks at the production, characteristics and uses of educational web sites designed for use in the home.

David Buckingham is Professor of Education at the Institute of Education, where he directs the Centre for the Study of Children, Youth and Media. He has conducted several research projects on children's interactions with electronic media and on media education.

Glimpses of educational transformation

Making choices at a turning point

Bridget S. Somekh
The Manchester Metropolitan University, 799 Wilmslow Road, M20 2RR, UK; b.somekh@mmu.ac.uk

Abstract: This paper is based on the study of four separate evaluations of the implementation of Information and Communication Technology (ICT) policies in schools in England during 1998-2002. The education system was in transition with new equipment coming into schools and patterns of computer use changing radically as a result of the Internet and school intranets. The most significant impact appeared to result from children's extended access to computers in the home. Children were using ICT in exploratory and innovative ways for leisure activities through which they were rapidly acquiring advanced skills. They also had the kind of sophisticated understanding of the role of computers in today's world that is a necessary condition of being able to envisage possible ways of using ICT for maximum benefit. The paper comes to the conclusion that a more radical approach to re-structuring the education system is necessary.

Key words: change, social contexts, sites of learning, policy, evaluation

1. INTRODUCTION

Between 1998 and 2002, a period of the steep upward curve in the exponential growth of technologies that started twenty or so years ago, digital technologies have entered the home and work lives of most people in the UK. The extraordinary shift in the patterns of human activity in the home and the workplace suggests that currently there are unparalleled opportunities for radical changes in schools and the education system. The system of schooling has proved resistant to reform in the last quarter century. The vision of politicians that technology would transform education has not so far been realised. Maybe we stand now at a turning point where there are two possible ways forward for the education system: Evolutionary change to the current system in line with larger changes in our society, or the sweeping away of schools as we know them to be replaced by an anarchic mix of online courses, student self-help and fragmentation of the state provision of education. What are the signs that our state education systems are capable of radical evolutionary change?

2. GOVERNMENT ICT-ORIENTED INITIATIVES

The UK government has invested heavily in networked technologies for schools in the last five years. Investment in the National Grid for Learning (NGfL), launched in 1998, totalled £657 million by 2002 and a further £710 million has been allocated to continue its development through 2002-4. In addition, £180 million was made available for teacher training through the New Opportunities Fund (NOF) (Somekh, et. al. 2001b). Progress was driven by a set of explicit targets: First, that all schools, colleges, universities and public libraries and as many community centres as possible would be connected to the NGfL by 2002; second, that Britain would become a centre of excellence in the development of networked software content.

Three other targets were also addressed: Ensuring the development of teachers' confidence and competence to teach using ICT; enabling school leavers to have a good understanding of ICT, with measures in place for assessing their competence in it; and a move to paperless communications between government and education bodies (DfES 2002). By 2001 the first targets had been almost achieved: 99 percent of secondary, 96 percent of primary and 97 percent of special schools were connected to the Internet. Seventy-one percent of secondary, 37 percent of primary and 33 percent of special schools had their own web sites (Somekh, et. al. 2001b). A consultation paper, published in May 2001 set out detailed proposals to consolidate progress on the second target. The NGfL portal was to be upgraded to establish a substantial resource of online educational materials, Curriculum Online (DfEE 2001). Although not all fully achieved, the five targets presented a coherent vision for increasing *use* of ICT in schools.

Alongside the investment in infrastructure and focus on achieving measurable targets, there has been a vision of entitlement to ICT as a means of increasing the life chances of all young people regardless of their families' socio-economic circumstances. David Blunkett, then Secretary of State for Education and Employment, said in a speech in 1998: "The involvement of the family in the learning process and the links between home and school are vital to the success we are seeking in raising standards and providing real equality of opportunity" (Pickering 2000). ICT was seen by government as a mechanism to link home and school and give parents and families access to educational materials. The E-Learning Foundation and Computers Within Reach were set up to place computers in the homes of disadvantaged families. To capitalise on the enthusiasm and motivation of children for ICT, in 2001 the DfEE set up a public-private partnership with strong links to the National Curriculum, partnering Channel 4 Television, Oracle Inc. and Intuitive Media to develop GridClub, "an educational fun site" for 7-11 year-olds.

Implementation of the policies has been monitored and evaluated by a series of government-funded research projects. This paper draws on four of them: ImpaCT2, the evaluation of the impact of ICT on students' attainment (co-directed by Colin Harrison, University of Nottingham, Peter Scrimshaw, Open University and Bridget Somekh, Manchester Metropolitan University); Pathfinders, the evaluation of the rollout of the NGfL in ten Pathfinder local education authorities (three strands led by Ros Sutherland, University of Bristol, Colin Harrison, University of Nottingham and Don Passey, University of Lancaster with Bridget Somekh, MMU as synoptic evaluator); ICTHOS, research into the use of ICT to enhance home-school links (Bridget Somekh, Diane Mavers and Cathy Lewin, MMU); and evaluation of the GridClub web site (Bridget Somekh and John Robinson, MMU, and Peter Scrimshaw, independent consultant).

3. THE IMPACT OF ICT ON EDUCATION

3.1 The education system in transition

Evidence from the ImpaCT2 project (Harrison, et. al. 2001; Harrison, et al. 2002) shows that during 2000-02 the education system was in transition. There was a time lag between the allocation of funds by central government and the installation of networks by the local education authority (LEAs) together with the arrival of new machines in schools. Some schools began to receive a significant amount of new equipment during 2000 but often the new machines were unfamiliar PCs replacing Acorn machines. Evidence from the Pathfinder evaluation (Somekh, et. al. 2001a; Somekh, et al. 2002) showed that some teachers who had been regular users of ICT saw that the move to PC networks in 2000 meant it was no longer possible to use "legacy" software. In primary schools stand-alone machines in individual classrooms were replaced by computer suites with an intranet connected to the Internet. For many primary schools the arrival of the intranet meant that they had to manage a server for the first time.

In their preliminary reports in March 2000, describing the use of ICT in their schools, the ImpaCT2 teacher-researchers revealed a mixture of excitement and frustration (Harrison, et al. 2002). There was an expectation that the new resource would be of great value but schools were disrupted by cable-laying and re-allocation of rooms to make space for suites. The tradition of ICT use was itself disrupted and new routines of use had not yet been established.

By 2002, networked technologies were becoming established in some schools and primary teachers were markedly more confident in their use, perhaps as a result of using ICT suites and working with a ratio of 2:1 computers per child (or sometimes 1:1) for the first time. However, schools continued to battle with the logistics of moving children and teachers to computer suites.

3.2 The school-based acquisition of ICT skills

It is assumed by the majority of teachers that children need to be taught ICT skills. The installation of computer suites in primary schools has made the teaching of skills much easier for teachers, many of whom still declare themselves to be tentative users of ICT. There is also a desire not to discriminate in favour of children who have computers at home, which has led to an institutional blindness to their home-based achievements (Somekh, et. al. 2001b). For some children skills teaching is unnecessary and probably dull.

The guidelines from the Qualifications and Curriculum Authority, used by many primary schools, encourage a pattern of use to ensure that schools enable children to achieve the National Curriculum attainment targets for ICT. Suggested lessons integrate the teaching of skills with authentic uses of ICT for learning. In practice, the data suggest that the emphasis of both teachers and children is on skills acquisition rather than using ICT to learn subject knowledge. From survey responses (Somekh, et al. 2002) it is clear that children believe that the purpose of using computers in school is to acquire skills and classroom observations (Somekh, et. al. 2001a) show that, even when teachers set out with the intention of using computers for subject learning, all their verbal interactions with children are about how to operate the computer rather than the topic of study identified in the lesson plan.

3.3 Considerable use of word processors

Both Pathfinders and ImpaCT2 research showed that the most frequent use of computers in primary schools was for word processing, which produced smart copies of writing, often for display purposes. However, ICTHOS pupils in a middle school (9-13 year-olds) were highly motivated by using their laptops for writing both at home and at school. The ImpaCT2 final report (Harrison, et al. 2002) recommended that teachers should have specialist training in using word processors as tools to improve writing rather than merely as presentational tools. Given their popularity in primary schools it seems certain that word processors could have a major impact on the quality of children's writing if teachers had a better understanding of how they could be used.

3.4 Learning difficult concepts

One of the glimpses of the power of ICT to transform learning was revealed in evidence from ImpaCT2. Six teacher researchers working with the 9-11 year old children described a variety of uses of ICT for science teaching (Harrison, et al. 2002). They emphasised the way ICT helped children learn difficult concepts:

> It was very beneficial because the interactive nature of CD-ROMs means that difficult concepts can be explained and if schools have limited resources, the children can observe a practical investigation taking place instead of just reading about it. The Internet can be also used to demonstrate practical investigations. Some software allows children to test their ideas and their outcome and change variables in the activity. Any gaps in the science curriculum are easy to fill like this or it's possible to revisit previous concepts — children enjoy this type of presentation. (Honeypot Lane Primary School)

3.5 Needing to read

Some of the ImpaCT2 teacher researchers reported in 2000-01 that it was difficult to use the Internet with primary-aged children if they did not have sufficiently good reading skills (Harrison, et al. 2002), a finding that may have very positive implications for learning. The Pathfinder evaluation showed a significant increase between 2000 and 2001 in the number of children who reported that computers "helped them with reading", coinciding with a significant increase in the levels of Internet use (Somekh, et al. 2002), giving another glimpse of the potential of ICT to transform learning. A "need to read" phenomenon may prove to be very beneficial in raising levels of achievement in reading. Boys may be able to engage in screen reading without arousing negative peer group pressure.

3.6 Innovative use of ICT in the home

ImpaCT2, Pathfinders and ICTHOS all provided considerable evidence of children's enthusiasm for using computers and the Internet in their own homes. This confirmed the findings from earlier work in Australia and the UK (Downes 1996; 1999; Sutherland, et al. 2000; Facer, et al. 2001). Accounts of their use of ICT at home, written by primary children for the Pathfinders project, showed a very wide range of innovative, exploratory activities, often carried out alone, but sometimes with the assistance of family or friends. Children reported a rather higher rate of things "going wrong" at home, often because they were attempting to accomplish tasks requiring high levels of technical skill — tasks that were potentially much more rewarding than the ICT-based work they were allowed to do at school (Somekh, et al. 2002).

In the GridClub evaluation, primary children working with the team as Young Evaluators have demonstrated extraordinarily high levels of expertise with ICT (Mavers 2002). On the rare occasions when we have been able to observe children engaging in innovative special ICT projects at school they have demonstrated their ability to work creatively at a very high level, both technically and conceptually. While "exceptional" children tend to be more likely to be offered exceptional opportunities, the evidence suggests that all children would benefit from being encouraged to use computers in the more open-ended ways they use them at home.

In the course of working with children in all four projects, both through formal data collection, informal conversations and collaborative work with children as researchers, it was clear that they are rapidly acquiring skills in the use of digital technologies. ImpaCT2 data showed that by June 2001 85 percent of 10-11 year olds had a computer at home and 66 percent were connected to the Internet. On average, children spend three times as long on ICT in the home as they do at school (Harrison, et al. 2002). Pathfinders data showed that children are engaging in challenging and innovative uses of ICT in the home for their own leisure purposes (Somekh, et al. 2002).

3.7 Play and games

The ImpaCT2 and Pathfinder surveys established that the most popular computer-based activity for children is "playing games". Most schools have rules forbidding games playing which means that children report less frequent games playing at school than at home.

The really interesting issue here is the power of games for learning. Adult assumptions about games being "mindless" need to be challenged. The Pathfinders survey data (Somekh, et al. 2002) shows a strong correlation between games playing and children's belief that computers "help" with some critically important mathematical skills such as "visualising 3-D images in your mind" and "calculating".

Many educational activities are presented to children in a games format. Often these are of poor quality and cannot compete for children's attention with the products they can buy on CD-ROM or download from the Internet. The GridClub portal, however, provides children with interactive games produced by media and software experts with a background in the entertainment industry <www.gridclub.com>. Although the evaluation of GridClub is not complete evidence suggests that the games provide powerful learning opportunities for children.

There is also evidence that researchers need to be very careful in interpreting children's answers to questions about "games" and "learning" in relation to their use of computers. Children's experience has taught them to make much cruder categorisations of their computer-based activities than researchers may realise. From their enculturation at school and at home children appear to assume that activities that are fun and enjoyable are "games"; and "learning" only refers to what teachers are teaching them at school. Hence one 10 year-old boy, who said that in one week he spent seven hours using a computer at home and one hour at school, at first categorised all his home use as "games". However his responses to further questions showed that they were games from which he would certainly have been learning something of value. For example, on Monday he said: "I went on the Internet and got pictures," and on Wednesday and Thursday he spent a total of two hours playing "a manager game" — "managing" the Liverpool football club. On Thursday he spent half an hour on a game called Sensible Soccer and on Friday he "played on a game where you could make your own music."

4. CONFLICTING POLICY INITIATIVES

The NGfL is only one of many UK policy initiatives for education. If it is not clear to teachers how the initiatives can be integrated, they compete with one another for time. ImpaCT2 teachers leading research activities in the school said they reduced the amount of time they spent using computers in their teaching as a result of two other initiatives introduced at around the same time: the National Numeracy Strategy (NNS) and the National Literacy Strategy (NLS). The recommended teaching methods for the NLS and NNS include a large element of "whole class teaching" with the teacher engaging all the children's attention from the front of the class. Teachers said they found the initiative's requirements incompatible with using ICT (Harrison, et al. 2001).

Under our present system, teachers need to ensure that children will be able to demonstrate that they have achieved National Curriculum attainment targets at the expected levels. Although the pressure is greatest for literacy and numeracy, the National Curriculum places an emphasis on the teaching of subject knowledge in preparation for national tests. The majority of teachers have given no consideration to the benefits that ICT offers as a means of supporting open-ended project work or exploratory creativity.

4.1 Challenges to educational tradition

In reporting that there was "no time" to use computers when preparing children for national tests, teacher researchers in ImpaCT2 were embodying a resistance in the education system to disruption of established traditions. The assumptions embedded in the assessment system are antithetical to the new opportunities that ICT offers for learning. Many teachers felt that it would be irresponsible to spend much time using computers when preparing children to be assessed on hand-written tests. It was not merely that traditional forms of assessment place emphasis on hand-writing and spelling, which are unimportant when using a computer; traditional forms of assessment also give no credit for the acquisition of new skills such as finding information on the Internet, selecting for relevance, down-loading, processing and presenting it. In fact, the skills raise major problems in relation to traditional forms of assessment, which have depended upon the production of hand-written scripts under examination conditions to prevent any possibility of "plagiarism" or "cheating". Yet, as a parent said when discussing plagiarism with a researcher in the ICT and Home-School Links project (ICTHOS): "It's perhaps a different approach to education — to assimilate what's outside there and put it together for the purpose in view. I think that's a higher level skill which doesn't develop at the same pace — a more subtle approach to learning" (Somekh , et. al. 2001b).

5. THE NEED FOR RADICAL CHANGE

The evidence from the four evaluation projects strongly suggests that there is a need for radical change in the education system. Too many assumptions in the present system work against the kind of transformation in schooling and learning which ICT makes possible and which is observable in children's use of ICT in the home. Until recently, NGfL policy has not aimed at radical change but at improving children's standards of attainment in the National Curriculum in the UK. The policy conflicts with the nature of digital technologies, which offer new ways of learning new things within different structures.

Currently there is an awareness among UK policy-makers of the need for more fundamental change, for example in discussion of "the school of the future" as the venue for an ICT-rich learning environment in the 21st century' (DfEE 2001). But we are dealing with long established traditions and in-built assumptions about teachers' and students' roles and responsibilities, the value of students' accumulating facts and skills through traditional whole class teaching, and the "gold standard" of high grades in a formal system of national tests and examinations, hand-written in silence without access to technology tools or interaction with others. Our society as a whole subscribes to many of these traditions. It will require considerable vision and courage to turn such a system around.

REFERENCES

DfEE (2001) *Curriculum Online - A Consultation Paper*. London: Department for Education and Employment.

DfES (2002) *Transforming the Way We Learn*. Norwich: Department for Education and Skills.

Downes, T. (1996) The computer as a toy and a tool in the home: Implications for schools and teachers. *Education and Information Technologies* 1 3/4 191-201.

Downes, T. (1999) Playing with computing technologies in the home. *Education and Information Technologies* 4 1 1-15.

Facer, K., Furlong, J., Sutherland, R. and Furlong, R. (2001) Home is where the hardware is: Young people, the domestic environment and 'access' to new technologies. In I. Hutchby and J. H. Moran-Ellis (eds.) *Children, Technology and Culture*. London: Falmer Press 13-27.

Harrison, C., Fisher, T., Haw, K., Lewin, C., McFarlane, A., Mavers, D., Scrimshaw, P. and Somekh, B. (2001) *ImpaCT2: Emerging Findings from the Evaluation of the Impact of Information and Communications Technologies on Pupil Attainment*. London: Department for Education and Skills.

Harrison, C., Fisher, T., Haw, K., Lewin, C., Mavers, D., Scrimshaw, P. and Somekh, B. (2002) ImpaCT2 Final Report (draft). Coventry: Becta.

Mavers, D. (2002) The Internet from a child's perspective. A paper presented at the IFIP Working Group 3.5 conference. Manchester, UK, June 29 -1uly 5, 2002.

Pickering, I. (2000) Whose child is it anyway? *Managing Schools Today*. November/December 2000 19-20.

Somekh, B., Barnes, S., Triggs, P., Sutherland, R., Passey, D., Holt, H., Harrison, C., Fisher, T., Joyes, G. and Scott, R. (2001a) *NGfL Pathfinders: Preliminary Report on the Roll-out of the NGfL Programme in Ten Pathfinder LEAs*. London: Department for Education and Skills.

Somekh, B., Mavers, D. and Lewin, C. (2001b) *Using ICT to Enhance Home-School Links: An Evaluation of Current Practice in England*. London: Department for Education and Skills.

Somekh, B., Barnes, S., Triggs, P., Sutherland, R., Passey, D., Holt, H., Harrison, C., Fisher, T., Flett, A. and Joyes, G. (2002) Second Preliminary Report on the Roll-out of the NGfL Programme in Ten Pathfinder LEAs (Draft).

Somekh, B. and Davies, R. (1991) Towards a pedagogy for Information Technology. *The Curriculum Journal* 2 2 153-170.

Sutherland, R., Facer, L., Furlong, R. and Furlong, J. (2000) A new environment for education? The computer in the home. *Computers and Education*. Special Edition 34 195-212.

BIOGRAPHY

Bridget Somekh has been researching the uses of ICT in education since 1984 when she experimented with using a computer to teach writing in her own classroom with 11-year-olds. She is currently Professor of Educational Research at Manchester Metropolitan University, UK. She has worked closely with teachers in collaborative Action Research projects and is an experienced evaluator of ICT programmes. Her books include *Using IT Effectively in Teaching and Learning: Studies in Pre-service and In-service Teacher Education* edited with Niki Davis (Routledge 1997) and *Teachers Investigate Their Work: An Introduction to the Methods of Action Research* co-authored with Herbert Altrichter and Peter Posch (Routledge 1993). In the last five years Bridget has been an invited keynote speaker on ICT in education at conferences in the USA, Brazil, Brussels (the European Commission), Hong Kong, Hungary, Norway, Portugal and Singapore. She is a member of IFIP's Working Group 3.5.

How do we know that ICT has an impact on children's learning?

A review of techniques and methods to measure changes in pupils' learning promoted by the use of ICT

Margaret J. Cox
King's College London, University of London, Stamford Street, London SE1 9NN, UK; MJ.Cox@kcl.ac.uk

Abstract: Over the past 30 years many studies have been conducted into the effects of Information and Communication Technologies (ICT) on pupils' learning. The methods used have ranged from intervention methods where the researchers have brought specific educational software into the classroom and used subject-based tests to large-scale studies using pre- and post-tests of pupils in many different classroom settings.

Previous reviews concerning the validity of educational research findings in ICT have revealed limitations regarding the generalisability of some results and the consistency of the findings due to a number of factors: e.g., using conventional tests which may not measure the specific learning which occurs from the use of ICT; or conducting small–scale case studies, sometimes with little analysis of the wider implications of the findings. Many research studies do not take account of the possible longer-term impact of ICT on learning, which may result from the consequent learner's reflections and metacognition. This paper reviews a range of research methods and results which have been used in the past, and considers the consistency, the limitations and the implications for future research into the effects of ICT on pupils' learning.

Key words: social contexts, learning styles, conditions for learning, research, evaluation

1. INTRODUCTION

During the past thirty years many educational studies have been conducted to investigate the effects of ICT on children's learning, yet there is still conflicting evidence about the impact ICT has on learning under what circumstances and in what settings. The earliest of the research studies took place in the 1960's and 1970's (e.g. Merrill 1975; Bork 1981), and were conducted when researchers introduced pupils to educational software in a university environment. In those studies learners did not use ICT in a normal classroom setting or within their subject curriculum, but were using software specifically designed to address specific conceptual difficulties in subjects such as science or mathematics. In other studies conducted in the 1970's, researchers investigated the effects of subject-based software on university students' learning in a curriculum setting but the measurement of the impact on learning was conducted through traditional pre- and post-tests with an assessment of experimental and control groups' performance on conventional end-of-year examinations. Laurillard (1987; 1994), who was evaluating such studies, found that the kinds of learning which were promoted by the use of subject- based simulations were different from deriving and solving equations, the ostensible measures of the tests.

Since those early research studies into the effects of ICT on learning, there have been many studies reported in the literature which have included meta-analyses of many small-scale projects (Niemiec, et al. 1987) as well as large-scale research projects investigating the effects of ICT on children's learning (Watson 1993). Recent studies investigate pupils' learning of concepts and skills using specifically dedicated programmed learning environments such as Integrated Learning Systems (Underwood, et al. 1996). The effectiveness and limitations of some of the methods to measure the impact on learning are considered in the following sections.

2. METHODS OF MEASURING THE EFFECTS ON LEARNING

There are two main groups of research methods that have been used to measure the effects of ICT on children's learning. Quantitative studies involve large numbers of children, where additional factors such as the quality of the teaching as well as the ages and backgrounds of the pupils might be expected to be cancelled out by using large enough cohorts of different ages in a range of schools and classes, with different teachers (e.g., Cox 1993). Qualitative case studies, on the other hand, are used to collect detailed data about those additional factors as well as the activities of each learner, the nature of the ICT being used and the context in which the learning takes place (e.g., Abbott 1999).

2.1 Quantitative methods

In order to measure effects of ICT on learning that can be considered as generalisable across the wider community of learners, many studies have been designed to measure changes in conceptual or procedural understanding during a time span of pre-ICT activity to the time when activity has been completed. Those quantitative studies require setting up experimental groups using ICT and control groups not using ICT. Both groups are tested before and after the learning activities, and again usually with a delayed post-test. One of the limitations of the method is that it is difficult to determine the ways in which the control group activities might also contribute uniquely to the learning of the pupils in that group and it is difficult to isolate the ICT effects on the experimental groups. For example, other factors might be influencing the learning of the pupils. Increased enthusiasm of the teachers using ICT, the novelty of the ICT experience, etc. may play a role in subsequent performance It is also difficult to design specific tests which will measure fairly the learning of the control and experimental learning groups as will be explained later. The limitations of large-scale studies have resulted in many researchers choosing to conduct smaller qualitative studies instead.

2.2 Qualitative methods

Qualitative methods usually involve conducting in-depth case studies of small groups of learners. The method enables detailed records to be kept of all the ICT-related activities, the contributions of the teacher, the other learning experiences of the pupils when using and not using ICT, and the range and extent of the ICT use of each individual learner. The approach enables the researchers to identify the relationships between the learning outcomes and the ICT activities more precisely than other types of research but does not always allow any more generalised findings to emerge (e.g., Watson 1993).

For example, when the findings of case studies are reported there are often many unanswered questions such as, "What is the influence of the whole school environment compared with another school?" and "Would other teachers' pupils have similar learning outcomes?" Other questions include: "Would the ICT activity have the same effect on pupils of a different age?" and "How would the input from parents and friends outside contribute to the pupils learning?" In any investigation, there are factors — teachers' pedagogies, teachers' epistemologies, teachers' attitudes, teachers' practices, learners' attitudes, learners' ICT abilities, the learning context, ICT education resources and ICT developments — which may need to be considered in any investigation.

The limitations of both quantitative and qualitative methods have resulted in two approaches being used to try to improve the validity of the results and the generalisability of the findings. Both approaches involve combining the methods.

2.3 Combining the methods

There are two ways of combining quantitative and qualitative methods. One way is to conduct a large-scale quantitative study, and then conduct case studies of a sub-sample of the cohorts to investigate the range of factors in more depth and to illuminate the large scale data. (e.g., Cox 1993; BECTa 2002). The range of assessment instruments and other techniques need to relate to the nature and types of learning which can be hypothesised for the study, and the relationship between the quantitative and qualitative evidence needs to be justified in terms of the aims of the investigation. The other way is to adopt a well-established approach that is used in many other areas of educational research as well as in other disciplines. Such research involves conducting a meta-analysis of a large number of published case studies and/or quantitative studies from which the results can then be generalised (e.g., Niemiec, et al. 1987).

The main limitations of this approach are the nature of ICT itself and the rapidly changing uses being made in education. The way of minimising the effect is to analyse many studies which have already been conducted within a limited time frame, e.g., during 2001. However, in order to achieve reliable and valid results, we should include evidence reported in many different countries and in many different languages. Even literature reviews in the field of ICT show that the evidence from non-English publications is rarely used to analyse impact results, a practice which is not followed in other disciplines.

Whichever approach is used to investigate the effects of ICT on children's learning, there are strategies that can help researchers achieve reliable results.

3. LEARNING OBJECTIVES

The first considerations which need to be made before investigating the effects of ICT on children's learning is to ask what kinds of learning we are trying to measure, and what we already know about the learning approaches and difficulties. Those considerations can usually be informed by what has already been identified by the relevant research community about the particular learning evidence and theories that might be relevant. For example, if a project is being set up to measure the effects of using Logo on pupils' understanding of mathematics, then the first stage is to review the literature about pupils' misconceptions and learning difficulties in mathematics. It is not uncommon to read a research paper about investigating the effects of ICT on children's learning of mathematics, language or science that does not first provide the past empirical evidence about children's understanding of the relevant concepts. In order to investigate the impact of ICT on children's learning we need first to identify the learning objectives.

3.1 Identifying learning objectives

During the last thirty years there has been a growing body of research into pupils' learning in many subjects. For example, in science there is extensive evidence about pupils' misconceptions caused by the everyday experiences which pupils have which cause cognitive conflicts with the scientists' views (Gallop 1992), and there are similar widely-known learning difficulties relating to particular theories in modern languages education (Sadeq 2002).

Although the effects of ICT on pupils' learning cannot always be predicted nor confined to traditional learning goals, previous research evidence of pupils' particular misconceptions can provide a reliable basis for identifying the particular learning difficulties which pupils might have. The first stage, however, is to identify what kinds of learning one is trying to measure. We can ask: "Is it an improvement in the understanding of particular concepts, or the acquisition of new skills, or the development of new competencies?" and "What is the expected balance between learning aspects of a subject and learning about the ICT environment itself?" as well as "Are the learning objectives achievable by the ages of pupils being studied?"

For example, a review of pupils' data-handling skills (Cox and Nikolopoulou 1998) showed that pupils' abilities to handle Boolean logic are dependent on their age. Therefore, if we were to research the effects of ICT on children's skills in searching the Internet, we would need to take those cognitive limitations into account when deciding on the tasks, the methods and the analysis. Similarly, if we were to investigate what the effects of using the World Wide Web have on pupils' acquisition of foreign language skills we would firstly need to study the relevant theories and empirical evidence about language acculturation, information searching skills, and the influence of perceptions and representations.

The next stage of determining if ICT is having an impact on children's learning is to identify which methods will most effectively measure impact and are likely to match learning objectives and/or achievements.

3.2 Matching the methods to learning objectives

Goals of early research studies often included what impact ICT had on pupils' learning of well known concepts and skills, and the effects of science simulations on students' understanding of science concepts (Cox 2000), for example. In many of the earlier studies, the methods used to measure the impact of ICT on learning were used to measure the same skills and knowledge acquired through traditional teaching and learning environments. For example, pre- and post-tests would be developed based on problem-solving tasks to measure pupils' abilities to solve problems provided via ICT. But the research findings showed that the kinds of learning which occurred might instead be predicting relationships, or being able to draw graphs of such relationships rather than solving the mathematical relationships which the tests addressed.

In the first ImpacT study (Cox 1993) five different measures were developed to assess the possible mismatch between methods used to measure the learning achievements and the actual achievements which might occur. The first measure was an ICT general paper-based test to assess whether the use of ICT in different subjects had increased their ICT knowledge. Although the test, based on the International Education Association study (Pelgrum and Plomp 1993), was designed to assess many different ICT skills, it could not measure ICT skills which the pupils may have developed such as drafting and redrafting documents or modelling in spreadsheets.

The second type of assessments were pre- and post-tests to measure ICT's contribution to pupils' general reasoning skills, which in turn might have had an effect on their subject-based learning. The third type of assessments were pre- and post-subject-based tests; e.g., in mathematics to measure gains in learning specific mathematical concepts and skills such as angles, division, and problem solving. Finally, there were two types of concept-specific tests: One to measure concepts which the pupils might learn using either ICT or a more traditional method, and the second to measure ICT-specific skills and concepts which could only be learnt *through* the uses of ICT.

The detailed analysis of the first ImpacT project findings showed that for the ICT-related specific skills, the only methods which revealed pupils' achievements were those which were specifically designed to measure ICT-related skills such as data handling (e.g., Cox and Nikolopoulou 1997). However for the largest ImpacT samples (N=2000), the less specific subject-based assessments revealed statistically significant findings for gains in subject knowledge.

In the very recent ImpaCT2 study (BECTa 2002), as well as using baseline mathematical and English tests to measure gains in achievements, the team also developed an innovative use of concept maps to measure the pupils' perceptions of ICT environments, and the importance of different ICT devices and applications.

In addition to the range of methods which need to be developed or adopted to measure the impact of ICT on pupils' learning there is also the fact that learning can be organised in many different ways, both inside and outside the formal school environment.

4. ORGANISATION OF THE LEARNING

In order to measure the impact of ICT on learning we need to take account of the learning environment, the way in which the activities occur and the way in which the learning is organised. The ways the learner as an individual, group learning or networks of learners, will influence the learning outcomes in different ways and should be considered as part of the learning environment.

4.1 Individual learning

Even though there is an increasing use of the Internet by learners and sometimes it is difficult to know when and if a learner is working on her/his own or collaboratively, there is still extensive use of non-networked learning activities where the learner can be assessed on an individual basis. In the case of large-scale quantitative studies different instruments can be developed to assess the pupils' learning, as indicated above, because other factors, which might also have an impact on learning, are minimised. However, in both large-scale quantitative studies and small case studies we cannot assume that the learning begins or ends with the particular ICT-based activity. There are many other ways in which the learning may be enhanced, not all of which relate specifically to the ICT experience.

Previous research into ICT and learning (e.g., Phillips 1988) and many studies in psychology have shown that after a learner engages in a particular activity he/she continues to reflect on that experience, and assimilation and reorganisation of knowledge can continue to occur. This means that when measuring the impact of ICT on children's learning we should take account of learning continuing some time after the activities have ended. Neglecting this facet of knowledge making is a weakness in some case studies where learning is only assessed during the activity itself and no account is taken of longer term assimilation or metacognition.

Research has also shown that the impact of an ICT activity on children's learning will be influenced by the ability to work within the medium. In other words, learning achievements may be influenced by the learners' ICT literacy skills. So two other factors need to be taken into consideration: (1) when assessing the impact of ICT on children's learning, we need to find out what kinds of ICT literacy skills are required and in what ways these are related to the actual tasks and activities; (2) we need to consider how the learner's ICT skills and literacies might change over time thereby changing the learning experience and the balance between ICT learning and, for example, subject-based learning. It is usually necessary to measure both types of learning in parallel, factors which apply to pupils who learn in groups as well as to individual learners.

4.2 Learning in Groups

It has been established for many years that pupils learn from each other and from adult guidance (Vygotsky 1978). In many situations, learning with ICT includes collaborative learning (e.g., Crook 1996). So learning can involve small groups of learners working on the same computer-based problem at the same time, *or* two or more learners collaborating asynchronously over the Internet, *or* children collaborating with experts by accessing web pages or e-mailing, *or* whole-class collaborations involving projects and interactive whole class teaching. In designing research projects we need to take account of the effects different types of collaborations may have on the individual learner in the immediate and the longer term by identifying learning experiences within the research's objectives.

5. CONCLUSIONS

The different research methods which have been briefly reviewed and the strategies proposed may ensure that research into the effects of ICT on children's learning will lead to reliable and generalisable results. Many other factors, shown in Figure 1, may also be important influences on learning. One of the most useful strategies for conducting well-substantiated research is to ensure that existing knowledge is considered and used in the planning of any investigation

REFERENCES

Abbott, C. (1999) The Internet, text production and the construction of identity: Changing use by young males during the early to mid 1990s. Unpublished Ph.D. thesis, King's College London, University of London.

BECTa (2001) ImpaCT2: Emerging findings from the evaluation of the Impact of Information and Communications Technologies on Pupil Attainment. London: DFES. http://www.BECTa.org.uk/ImpaCT2

Bork, A. (1981) *Learning with Computers*. Bedford, MA: Digital Press.

Cox, M.J. (1993) Information Technology resourcing and use. In D. Watson (ed.) ImpacT - An evaluation of the Impact of the Information Technology on Children's Achievements in Primary and Secondary Schools. London: Kings College London.

Cox, M.J. and Nikolopoulou, K. (1997) What information handling skills are promoted by the use of data analysis software. Education and Information Technologies 2 105-120.

Cox, M.J.(2000) Information and Communication Technologies: Their role and value for science education.. In Monk, M., and Osborne, J.O. (eds.) *Good Practice in Science teaching. What Research Has to Say.* Buckingham: Open University Press UK.

Crook, C. (1994) *Computers and the Collaborative Experiences of Learning*. London: Routledge.

Laurillard, D.M. (1987) *Ed. Interactive Media: Working Methods and Practical Applications*. Chichester: Ellis Horwood.

Merrill, P.F. (1975) The role of computer technology in an open learning environment. Proceedings of the Second National Conference on Open Learning and Non-traditional Study 323-326.

Niemiec, R., Samson, G., Weinsten, T., and Walberg, H.J. (1987) The effects of computer based instruction in elementary schools: A quantitative synthesis. *Journal of Research on Computing in Education* 20 85-103.

Pelgrum, W.J., and Plomp, T (1993) *The IEA Study of Computers in Education: implementation of an innovation in 21 education systems.* Oxford: Pergamon Press.

Phillips, R. (1988). Four types of lesson with a microcomputer. *Micromath* 4 1 35-38: 4 2 7-11.

Sadeq, T. The contribution of Computer Assisted Language Learning to low achievers' learning of English as a foreign language. Unpublished Ph.D. thesis. King's College London, University of London.

Underwood, J., Cavendish, S., Dowlikng, S., Foogelman, K., and Lawson, T. (1996) Are integrated learning systems effective learning support tools? *Computers & Education* 26 1-3 33-40.

Vygotsky, L.S. (1978) *Mind in Society*. Cambridge, MA: Harvard University Press.

Watson D. (ed.) (1993) The ImpacT Report - An evaluation of the impact of Information Technology on children's achievements in primary and secondary schools. King's College London.

BIOGRAPHY

Margaret Cox is Professor of Information Technology at King's College London (University of London) and Honorary President of the Association for ICT in Education. She pioneered the use of Computer Assisted Learning

(CAL) at Surrey University in the early 1970's and published many papers on the contribution of CAL to students' learning. After several years as coordinator for Computer Assisted Learning at Surrey University, she became a faculty member at Chelsea College (now subsumed into King's College) and directed the Computers in the Curriculum Project, one of the largest projects developing and evaluating educational software, from 1982 to1991. During that period she also directed many other projects, including the ImpacT Project (with Professor David Johnson, also an IFIP member), the Economic and Social Research Council (ESRC) uptake of IT in primary schools' project, and the Modus project which designs and evaluates computer-based modelling in education. Her current research interests include the impact of ICT on children's learning, computer-based modelling in education, motivation, and the effects of professional development on teachers' pedagogical practices. She was awarded the OBE in 2001 for her contributions to IT in Education.

Index